D1512208

Washington's
FAREWELL

1 2 3 4 5 6 7 8 9 10 XXX 06 05 04 03 02 01 00 99

Library of Congress Cataloging-in-Publication Data
Murray, Stuart, 1948-
Washington's Farewell to his Officers: after victory in the Revolution/Stuart Murray.
p. cm.
Includes bibliographical references and index.
ISBN 1-88459-220-1 (cloth)

1. United States—History—Revolution, 1775-1783—Campaigns. 2. United States—History—Revolution, 1775-1783—Biography. 3. Evacuation Day, Nov. 25, 1783. 4. Washington, George, 1732-1799. 5. Farewells—New York (State)—New York. 6. New York (N.Y.)—History—Revolution, 1775-1783. I. Title.

E230 .M87 1999
973.3'3 21-dc21

99-043620

Copyright© 1999 Stuart Murray
Published by Images from the Past, Inc.,
P.O. Box 137, Bennington, VT 05201
Tordis Ilg Isselhardt, Publisher

Printed in the United States of America

Design and Production: Ron Toelke Associates, Chatham, NY
Printer: Thomson-Shore, Inc., Dexter, MI

Washington's

FAREWELL

TO HIS OFFICERS

AFTER VICTORY IN
THE REVOLUTION

STUART MURRAY 1948

Images from the Past
Bennington, Vermont

By arrangement with The Aberdeen Group, LLC

To the Monson Family

Irene, Chris, Christopher, Kim,
Drew, Amy, and Adam

CONTENTS

"'Tis ours for ever, from this hour to part,

Accept the effusions of a grateful heart!

Where'er you go, may milder fates pursue,

Receive my warmest thanks, my last adieu."

Swords turned to shares, and war to rural toil,

The men who saved, now cultivate the soil.

In no heroic age, since time began,

Appeared so great the majesty of man.

David Humphreys
Aide-de-camp to General Washington

From "Happiness of America,"
commemorating the farewell to the army in 1783.

PREFACE

It is not known who all the men were at George Washington's farewell to his officers at Fraunces Tavern in New York City in December of 1783.

The officers whose stories are within these pages must stand for all their comrades-in-arms who fought alongside them and General Washington in the War for American Independence.

It is the author's sincere hope that, in some small way, this work might brighten our image of every one.

Stuart Murray
East Chatham, New York

It only remains for the Commander in Chief to address himself once more, and that for the last time, to the armies of the United States…and to bid them an affectionate, a long farewell.

General George Washington
from Rocky Hill, near Princeton, New Jersey,
in a final message to his disbanded army,
November 1783

*After a painting by Charles Willson Peale of Washington
at the end of the Revolutionary War.*

New-York, Nov. 24, 1783.

The Committee appointed to conduct the Order of receiving their Excellencies Governor CLINTON and General WASHINGTON,

BEG Leave to inform their Fellow-Citizens, that the Troops, under the Command of Major-General KNOX, will take Poffeffion of the City at the Hour agreed on, Tuefday next ; as foon as this may be performed, he will requeft the Citizens who may be affembled on Horfeback, at the Bowling-Green, the lower End of the Broad-Way, to accompany him to meet their Excellencies GovernorCLINTON and General WASHINGTON,at the Bull's Head, in the Bowery---the Citizens on Foot to affemble at or near the Tea-water-Pump at Frefh-water.

ORDER OF PROCESSION.

A Party of Horfe will precede their Excellencies and be on their flanks---after the General and Governor, will follow the Lieutenant-Governor and Members of the Council for the temporary Government of the Southern Parts of the State---The Gentlemen on Horfe-back, eight in Front---thofe on Foot, in the Rear of the Horfe, in like Manner. Their Excellencies, after paffing down Queen-Street, and the Line of Troops up the Broadway, will a-light at CAPE's Tavern.

The Committee hope to fee their Fellow-Citizens, conduct themfelves with Decency and Decorum on this joyful Occafion.

CITIZENS TAKE CARE!!!

THE Inhabitants are hereby informed, that Permiffion has been obtained from the Commandant, to form themfelves in patroles this night, and that every order requifite will be given to the guards, as well to aid and affift, as to give protection to the patroles : And that the counterfign will be given to THOMAS TUCKER, No. 51, Water Street ; from whom it can be obtained, if neceffary.

A public notice announcing Washington's entrance into New York.

Evacuation

Day

Tuesday, November 25, 1783

A FLAG ON FORT GEORGE

*T*HE LAST BRITISH REDCOATS LINGERED on the docks at the lower tip of York Island, in no hurry to get into a boat waiting to row them to Royal Navy warships anchored in Hudson's River. It was mid-afternoon on a blustery autumn day, the water glittering with sunlight as many boatloads of soldiers made their way out to the ships. The American Revolution was won and lost, and the redcoats who had held New York City for King George the Third during seven long years were now departing in defeat.

Once the winds and tides were fair, the fleet would leave its anchorage and put to sea, carrying away more than six thousand British troops and several thousand "refugees," as American loyalists were now termed. The redcoats would be stationed elsewhere in the empire, but the loyalists found themselves on the losing side of a bitter civil war, and so were leaving their homeland forever.

There was something strange about this departure, however, because on the flagpole in nearby Fort George the British flag still snapped in the wind. For some reason, the flag had not been struck; and for some reason not all those longboats full of soldiers were heading directly for the ships. Sailors at the oars were pulling only slowly and—like the soldiers yet on the docks—seemed to be waiting for something, watching. Thousands of American spectators had gathered on York Island and over on the New Jersey shore to see the final departure of the occupying army. These people, too, all saw the British flag still flying on that flagpole in the northwest bastion of the fort.

Then the shrill of approaching American fifes and the rattle of their drums rang out from the city streets. The redcoats on the docks paused to look. Sailors in boat after boat out on the water rested on their oars, they and their redcoats turning to see what would happen next. Also watching were the British soldiers a few hundred yards away on Governor's Island, not yet evacuated, its own flag flapping. The American fifes played a familiar melody that rose above the marching drums. The British called it "God Save the King," but they knew the American words were "God Save Great Washington." This was General George Washington's victorious army entering the city, its advance guard marching in to raise the Stars and Stripes over Fort George. The Americans would be surprised to see the flag still flying there, because intentionally leaving a British flag over a surrendered fort, where it might be dishonored, was unheard of. Unheard of, too, was the defeat of the world's greatest military power by an army that had been mostly amateurs.

The column of American soldiers swung into the fort, flags flying, drums resounding across the water. Their weather-beaten uniforms looked drab compared to the brilliance of the redcoats, but the patriots were soldierly, fit, and strong. They marched well, briskly occupying the battery between the fort's walls and the water line, then hauling several polished brass field guns down there. These guns would be fired in salute when the American flag went up the pole.

First, of course, that redcoat flag had to come down.

The British onlookers could see American officers

approach the flagpole and hesitate, as if confused. This was the moment the redcoats had been waiting for: that flag would never be lowered. It had been nailed to the pole. Further, the halyard had been removed, and until the Americans replaced it, they had no way to raise their own flag. There was more: the flagpole's lower cleats had been knocked off, preventing anyone from climbing up to grab the British standard.

As the officers wondered what to do next, out of the crowd stepped John Van Arsdale, identifiable by his tarpaulin cap and short jacket as a sailor. Stocky and agile, in his late twenties, Van Arsdale offered to go up the flagpole. The officers agreed, and he sprang at the pole, wrapping his legs and arms around it, but soon he slid right down. The British in the boats howled with laughter, knowing the pole had been greased with tallow. Van Arsdale tried again and again, but slipped down each time. Even an experienced sailor could not get up to tear down the flag.

The few redcoats on the docks observed all this, smirking, but were cautiously silent. They dawdled a bit longer to watch as this final and most symbolic moment of victory in the American Revolution seemed about to be ruined by a crude soldier joke. Not until the Stars and Stripes flew above Fort George could the Americans fire their cannon in salute and officially take possession of New York. Moreover, the sound of that salute would signal General Washington and his procession of officers with their staffs and bodyguard, all waiting north of the city, to begin the entry. It would be His Excellency's last military ceremony as commander-in-chief, but a greased flagpole now threatened to deny him the full glory of this moment. Infuriated, one of the Americans planted a short staff with a Stars and Stripes into the earth of the fort's ramparts and exclaimed that this was good enough. An officer apparently agreed, and cannon began to fire their salute, the blasts echoing across city and bay.

But, no, the superior officers declared, this would not do at all, and they ordered the firing stopped after three or four shots. As long as the British flag flew high on that bedeviling staff, the Americans would not allow their Stars and Stripes to take an inferior position. There were angry shouts to get an axe, and chop the damned flagstaff down.

HIS EXCELLENCY,
GENERAL WASHINGTON

THE CANNON REPORTS CARRIED TWO miles away to the Bull's Head Tavern, on the northern edge of New York City, where General Washington was anticipating the thirteen blasts in salute to the raising of the American flag over Fort George. The time had come for the procession to begin.

Throughout eight long years fighting an almost unwinnable war, Washington had devoted his life to this moment. Even after the great victory over Cornwallis at Yorktown in October 1781 he had refused to declare the war as won. It would not be finished, he had insisted, until the last British soldier departed the United States for good. That required keeping an American army in the field for two more years and sustaining its will to fight even though neither rebels nor British were actively campaigning. It meant being

Washington and his entourage entering New York City
on Evacuation Day, November 25, 1783.

ever watchful that the empire did not suddenly, unexpectedly, hurl its military weight more forcefully than ever against the former colonies. Since the announcement of the final peace terms in the spring, Washington had been waiting for the British and their loyalists to evacuate New York City, the last enemy stronghold on the eastern seaboard.

Much of those two uncertain years after Yorktown had been spent confined in lonely winter encampments up Hudson's River, a chapter of the war dominated by the struggle to keep an army in existence lest the British detect weakness or disunity and refuse to make a real peace. Washington's task had been all the more difficult because he had to contend with the mean-spirited politics and regional jealousies of the Continental Congress, which had not adequately paid the officers and men since Yorktown. Only the general's force of will and the love his men felt for him had sustained the army so long.

Even now, Congress balked at paying the troops. This past summer it had ordered Washington to furlough most of his force, regiment by regiment, unceremoniously sending them home with only their muskets, a certificate of partial payment, and a vague promise that they would be paid in full someday. The troops were dispersed quietly, as if going on leave, thus reducing the risk of mutiny, riot, or a march on Congress to demand back pay. So the valiant Continental Army simply melted away, with little formality, with even less thanks from Congress. After all they had done for America, many of the soldiers were left destitute, going home embittered and embarrassed, too often to be thrown on the charity of communities they had fought to make independent. Nor was that charity always forthcoming.

While for Washington the entry into New York was a moment of high drama and personal satisfaction, all was not as joyful as it seemed. Congress's betrayal of his army, of the men and officers who had trusted his assurances that they would be paid before being dismissed, was deeply troubling to him. For the moment, however, there was this most enjoyable ceremony to be attended to. Charged by Congress in 1775 with "the maintenance and preservation of American liberty," he had sworn to see the war through to its final scene. Not before this day would he allow himself to go home to Virginia and his beloved Mount Vernon, which he had been able to visit only once during the entire war. Today, the Revolution really was finished.

Washington had succeeded at last, against all the odds.

Yet, as he and New York's governor, George Clinton, and their entourage prepared to enter the city, it seemed something was not quite right, for the cannon reports had stopped. There had not been the full thirteen. By now, the imposing, brick-built Bull's Head Tavern was surrounded by swarms of jubilant New Yorkers eager for a look at His Excellency. The people cheered when he and Clinton mounted their horses to ride through the noisy crowd and down Bowery Lane. Followed by officers and state officials, also on horseback, Washington expected soon to meet his second in command, Major-general Henry Knox, at the head of a mounted welcoming delegation of prominent citizens, some of them former officers of the Continental Army.

This entry was not, however, New York City being taken over by the Continental Army. It was not even George Washington's triumphal parade at the head of conquering troops. Instead, Washington was here as the honored guest of

Governor Clinton and the State of New York. The troops were under the direct command of Clinton and Knox, not Washington, who was soon to submit his resignation to Congress. First, the general would see to it that civil authority returned to New York, consistent with his overriding precept that military rule must always be subordinate to, and yield to, civilian rule. He and the army were here mainly to ensure the city's safe and peaceful transition to independence and civilian rule. No rioting would be allowed, no wholesale attacks on those who had remained in the city during the British occupation. There would be no lawless grab for property that had been abandoned by loyalist refugees (as many as forty thousand from several states had fled through New York to other British possessions or to Britain).

On such a festive occasion, known as "Evacuation Day," Washington was grateful to be relatively unencumbered with

The Bull's Head Tavern, where Washington waited in preparation for entering New York City after the British had left.

day-to-day duties. Let someone else manage the army now and take the organizational responsibility. He could savor this long-anticipated closing to the war.

Out on Bowery Lane there was a hearty greeting between the entourage of Washington and Clinton and Knox's party, many old friends being happily reunited. The welcoming delegation from New York all wore "a badge of distinction" pinned on their chests, a cockade made of black and white ribbon to celebrate the American alliance with France. They also wore a laurel sprig in their hats, symbol of victory and peace. The crowd of New Yorkers took delight in seeing these famous men in person, men whose names and deeds they had often heard about during the siege: Washington, the brothers George and James Clinton, Knox, Steuben, McDougall, Van Cortlandt, Lamb, Jackson, Hull, Hamilton, Fish, Varick, Tallmadge.... Many were sons of their own city and state.

The procession formed a column and set off into town, turning right from Bowery Lane onto the cobblestones of Chatham Street and led by a vanguard of militia horsemen from Westchester County. Washington was next, tall and straight in the saddle and dressed in the dark blue coat and buff smallclothes of a Continental general officer. On his spirited gray mount, he looked every bit the unsurpassed horseman he was said to be. During the most crucial battles of the war, he had practically lived in the saddle, on horseback for days at a time, tirelessly appearing at the side of his men, seeming everywhere at once. Governor Clinton, riding a fine bay beside Washington, was himself a handsome figure as they rode on, followed by a few senior officers and their aides, then by Knox and the civilian riders. The Westchester Light Horse flanked each side of the column.

As Washington's procession passed along Chatham Street, ever larger crowds appeared, cheering, waving, and applauding, happy folk on every side. For all the excitement, though, this was not the huge, impressive parade it might have been, with dozens of proud regiments and thousands of grinning heroes praised for their astonishing victory. After the disbandment of the army, the troops remaining to march into New York with Washington numbered only eight hundred. Composed of New York artillery and Massachusetts infantry, they had been reorganized and officially designated the First American Regiment. Earlier in the day, the main body of soldiers had marched with Knox into the city, following just yards behind the rear column of withdrawing redcoats. The Americans had sent patrols throughout the town to prevent civil disturbances while the rest of the troops and the artillery had gone down to Fort George to raise the Stars and Stripes.

Still, the thirteen cannon firing from that fort had not been heard. Had something gone wrong?

A contemporary view of Fort George.

*N*o AMERICAN WANTED the final ceremony of the war to be like this, but that insolent flag and the greased flagpole were giving the redcoats the last laugh.

There should correctly have been a British color guard and officers present to meet the arrival of the Americans at Fort George. Then the flag would have been politely lowered to the roll of drums and the playing of a British anthem with all formality and respect. That would have been followed by the Stars and Stripes rising to the salute of American cannon.

Then there came an idea, and men hustled away to an ironmonger's shop at Hanover Square to fetch nails and tools; others split a board that could be cut up to serve as cleats for climbing the pole. Something had to be done, and quickly, for His Excellency would appear soon—too soon. If the British flag were not lowered, the Stars and Stripes not raised in time, Washington, Clinton, New York, and all the United States would be embarrassed. Out in the harbor were French and American ships, their own national standards fluttering, everyone aboard waiting for the proud moment when the American flag would fly over the city, and the guns fire triumphantly.

It was infuriating. Someone had to get up that pole and yank off the hated British flag. In the meantime, the last redcoats clambered into their longboat, enjoying themselves under the circumstances—circumstances that otherwise were about as miserable as possible for the British Army.

THE PROCESSION

*F*OR WASHINGTON, MEMORIES OF OTHER DAYS in New York were awakened on every side as he rode along crowded Chatham Street, with its brick houses and red tile roofs. After years of siege and hardship, the place was squalid, most houses run down, windows boarded up, doors of green and red and blue in need of paint.

Most of the trees had been chopped down for firewood, and once-bustling warehouses stood shattered and empty, littered with rubbish from the soldiers who had been quartered there. Those warehouses had been built in a time of peace and prosperity, when free commerce had kept them stocked with the empire's goods, which had enriched the city. New York had been thriving when Washington came here back in 1775 on his way to Boston as commander of the new Continental Army. With the finest and most convenient harbor on the coast, the city was prosperous and bustling despite years of British trade regulations.

Even by 1783, Washington, the genteel Virginia planter and conscientious slave owner, did not understand New York, did not know what to think of its consuming passion for money-making, relentless bargaining, and quick profit. He considered the city an immoral, loose, and restless place run by an ambitious class of middling, irreverent merchants. Back in 1775, Washington had expected unruly, freewheeling New York to become a hotbed of loyalism, no matter whose military occupied it. In some ways he had been right, for its citizens did not hate English rule on principal as Boston did, nor was it jealous of London's supremacy, as was Philadelphia, which had been the second-greatest city in the empire. Insurrection, war, and independence did not seem to bode well for business-minded New Yorkers, who had always prospered from imperial commerce. Yet, from the city and state rose up many of the strongest advocates of American independence.

New York had provided the rebel forces with resolute fighting men and several of the best officers, a number of whom were in His Excellency's procession today. Many of the people now cheering from windows, doorways, and up on rooftops were recently returned "exiles," as rebels who had fled the city during the occupation were called. They had come back to rebuild their lives, but they often found their homes and shops in ruins, for no other American city had suffered as much as New York had during the eight grinding years of war and siege.

After forcing the British Army to abandon Boston in the spring of 1776, Washington had returned to New York as the conquering hero. On July 9 of that year, he had ordered the newly adopted Declaration of Independence read aloud to the entire army, which had paraded in various camps in and around the city. The two brigades assembled in the Commons had heard a regimental chaplain read parts of the 80th Psalm during the ceremony.

> *Thou hast brought a vine out of Egypt: thou hast*
> *cast out the heathen and planted it.*
> *Thou preparedst room before it, and didst cause it*
> *to take deep root, and it filled the land.*

> *The hills were covered with the shadow of it, and*
> > *the boughs thereof were like the goodly cedars.*
> *She sent out her boughs unto the sea, and her*
> > *branches unto the river.*

The 80th Psalm had profound meaning to an America that had been prospering for a century and a half until conflict with the British government brought on harsh trade regulations and bitter civil strife and stifled commerce with the rest of the world. Then the coming of war had virtually closed down the eastern seaboard to all but military shipping. The psalm asked what was to become of America now? As it was intoned, a sudden thundershower had swept in, summer lightning crashing all around, and fat raindrops spattering the troops, who remained stoically in rank.

> *Why hast thou then broken down her hedges, so*
> > *that all they which pass by the way do pluck her?*
> *The boar out of the wood doth waste it, and the*
> > *wild beast of the field doth devour it.*
> *Return, we beseech thee, O God of hosts: look*
> > *down from heaven, and behold, and visit this vine.*
> > > * * *
> *O Lord God of hosts, cause thy face to shine;*
> > *and we shall be saved.*

*T*HE RAINSTORM HAD PASSED as swiftly as it had come, but at the very moment Washington's army was listening to the psalm and the reading of the Declaration of Independence, another kind of storm was gathering: one of the mightiest

British fleets ever assembled was anchoring in New York Bay. There were ten towering ships of the line, twenty frigates, and more than two hundred transports carrying thirty-two thousand troops. On those first days of independence, Washington's twenty thousand optimistic, untested American soldiers never imagined how in the next half year they would be defeated again and again, to be forced out of New York City for the rest of the war. The general would be ever scheming to get back in.

The night the Declaration of Independence was proclaimed in the city, a gilded lead equestrian statue of King George III was pulled by a mob from its pedestal on the Bowling Green and torn apart to be turned into thousands of rebel musket balls. Washington was sorry to see such wanton destruction. He once had hoped the king and Parliament would not push America into civil war and revolution. By July 1776, even though that huge British invasion force was poised to attack, Washington believed vigorous resistance and stubborn defensive warfare would prove to the king that it was not worth fighting a long and costly war to prevent American independence.

Instead of successfully resisting the invasion, however, Washington's army suffered its worst defeats of the entire war in and around New York that year. He was outmaneuvered, pummeled, beaten, and driven out, his crumbling army barely escaping to fight again. For the rest of the war New York served the enemy well, a dagger pointed at the American heart, a center for espionage and the refuge of thousands of fleeing loyalists who exhorted the British Army to prosecute the war and destroy Washington and Congress.

If Congress had not objected to it, Washington would have

burned New York to the ground to prevent the British from using the city as their main base. As it turned out, he was pleased when four days after the rebels had withdrawn, someone started a fire that laid waste to much of the southwest corner of the city

𝓑 Y THE TIME WASHINGTON'S PROCESSION was met by an official delegation of city men near Chatham Square, there still had been no more cannon fire from Fort George. The delegation offered congratulations and praise for the general and Clinton, and when the formalities were finished, the parade continued, larger now by the addition of the officials.

Behind Washington and Clinton rode Lieutenant-governor Philip Van Cortlandt and the members of the temporary city council, four abreast; then came Major-general Knox and the officers of the army, retired and active, followed by prominent citizens on horseback, all riding eight abreast; the rest of the state and city officials followed on foot, also eight across.

Where Queen Street led off southward from Chatham Street, Washington and Clinton drew to one side, along with their staffs and the mounted citizens, as Knox and the officers cantered on ahead down Chatham Street toward the Commons and Broadway. Here, Washington's party turned onto Queen Street, following a parade route that was less direct than that taken by Knox and the others. This lengthened His Excellency's procession and gave Knox more time to prepare for the reception at Cape's Tavern on Broadway. It also prevented Washington's having to look at so many blackened and burned-out hulks of once-handsome buildings on

Broadway. There had been two fires during the occupation: the Great Fire in September 1776, immediately after Washington had been driven out, and the second in August 1778, farther to the southeast and not as severe. Together, these fires destroyed or damaged as many as eight hundred structures in the city.

The parade approached Hanover Square, near some of the buildings charred in the second fire, then turned right onto Wall Street. Washington was familiar with this part of town. If he had continued straight ahead from Queen Street, he would have entered Dock Street, passing by Fraunces Tavern, also known as The Queen's Head, where he would stay while in New York. Washington was acquainted with proprietor Samuel Fraunces, who had served the patriot cause in a number of ways, including offering kindness to captive rebels held in the city. Washington happened to be looking for a steward

The Fraunces Tavern building as it looked soon after being built by the DeLancey family in the early 1700s.

to manage the Mount Vernon household, and Fraunces would make a good one.

The procession rode up Wall Street, a long rise toward Broadway. Here were some of the city's finest houses, but they, too, were dilapidated and miserable because of too many soldiers garrisoned too close together for much too long. The best homes in this neighborhood had been commandeered as quarters for top officers of the king, including New York's military governor, General James Robertson, and the German generals, Knyphausen and Von Riedesel. The notorious Benedict Arnold, who as a rebel general had defeated Von Riedesel in battle, had lived nearby after betraying the rebel cause and his friend George Washington in the fall of 1780.

The British left the city a sad legacy of neglect, especially in the last year when the garrison was marking time, knowing it would have to depart. Civil government had broken down, and the army had no intention of repairing or maintaining

property that would be surrendered to the Americans. The streets were strewn with trash and filth, much of it lying there still on Evacuation Day. Not a shade tree remained on Wall Street, though once they had been numerous and stately. Like the trees, most wooden fences had been turned to firewood, even those enclosing churchyards and cemeteries. Many churches had been seriously damaged by the occupation, some converted into hospitals and prisons, others used as barracks and storehouses and even riding schools. Often,

The battered statue of former prime minister William Pitt near Wall Street.

the pews and galleries had been torn out and windows broken. Church graveyards were turned into rubbish dumps.

On Wall Street, Washington rode past a headless marble statue of William Pitt the Elder, the former British prime minister who had opposed the parliamentary policies that brought on the war. Erected in 1770 by the colonial assembly, which also gave the equestrian statue of the king that year, Pitt's statue depicted the prime minister in a Roman-style toga. Both tributes were erected in honor of the repeal of the hated Stamp Act in 1766, when there was a short-lived time of hope that relations between Britain and her American colonies would improve. It was said that British soldiers and royalists had knocked off the head of Pitt's statue because he opposed the war; but it was also said that rebellious Americans who considered Pitt a failure had done their share of the damage well before the redcoats arrived. On Wall Street, too, was handsome City Hall, which had been looted

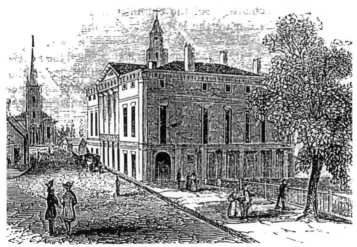

New York City Hall on Wall Street.

by British troops, who even stole its library's books to sell them. The building had been made a bleak prison for rebels.

As he was about to turn right from Wall Street onto Broadway, Washington faced the wreck of Trinity Church, which had been at the center of the Great Fire of 1776. Although the church was in ruins, the grounds had been styled a fashionable promenade by the British, who had held open-air concerts performed by garrison musicians and illuminated by lamps hung in charred tree limbs. From here, the general rode slowly past the ranks of the First American Regiment, which was standing smartly at attention in his and Clinton's honor. This would be George Washington's last review of Revolutionary troops.

Riding past the soldiers, His Excellency and Governor Clinton dismounted at Cape's Tavern on the west side of Broadway to be formally welcomed by "The Address of the Citizens of New York who have return'd from Exile, in behalf of themselves and their Suffering Brethren." The exiles had one uneasy eye on the British fleet anchored in the harbor, its pennants and ensigns flying:

> Sir: At a moment when the arm of tyranny is yielding up its fondest usurpations, we hope that salutations of long-suffering exiles, but now happy freemen, will not be deemed an unworthy tribute. In this place, and at this moment of exultation and triumph, while the ensigns of slavery still linger in our sight, we look up to you, our deliverer, with unusual transports of gratitude and joy. Permit us to welcome you to this city, long torn from us by the hard hand of oppression, but now by your wisdom and energy, under the

guidance of Providence, once more the seat of peace and freedom.... [W]e who now have the honor to address Your Excellency have often been companions of your sufferings and witness of your exertions... [Accept] our sincere and earnest wishes that you may long enjoy that calm domestic felicity which you have so generously sacrificed; that the cries of injured liberty may never more interrupt your repose, and that your happiness may be equal to your Virtues.

With quiet dignity, Washington listened to these words, but the guns at Fort George, a few hundred yards away, had not yet fired the expected salute to signal that the American flag had been raised.

*T*HE PEOPLE WAITING AT FORT GEORGE battery could hear the roars as Washington passed through nearby streets on his way to Cape's Tavern. It had been more than half an hour since the

The Fort George battery and the Bowling Green.

American troops first arrived here, but the tools for fixing wooden cleats to the pole still had not been found. For His Excellency's sake more than anything else, John Van Arsdale and the others wanted that flag pulled down and the Stars and Stripes run up.

These days Van Arsdale was employed as a sailor (the profession he had been brought up to as a boy), but he had served in the Continental Army for much of the war. In 1778 he had received a leg wound, was captured, and languished in prison for some months before being exchanged. He resumed service as a soldier until discharged along with most of the troops earlier this year. Recently married, he was glad to have found work as an able seaman on the *Black Prince,* a former rebel gunboat fitted out as a freighter plying Hudson's River. He had come up here from the docks and joined the crowd, hoping to see Washington one last time before the general set off for Virginia, likely gone forever from New York.

Then the tools came, stirring the gloomy crowd, giving

Redcoats crowd into a boat as they are evacuated from New York City and taken to waiting ships.

them hope as Van Arsdale began to nail the wooden slats to the flagpole, working himself higher and higher. It was laborious and difficult to nail securely into a round flagpole with only one's legs to hang on with while both hands did the work. Though there was no time to waste—the cheering for Washington seemed closer than ever—it was slow going, especially in the teeth of a cold northwester.

Unexpectedly, a long ladder was brought and set against the flagpole. It did not reach all the way up, but was enough to get almost to the topmost cleats, which the redcoats had not bothered to knock off. With a halyard stuck in his belt, Van Arsdale scampered up the ladder as spectators shouted encouragement. From the top rung he got to the cleats and pulled himself up the rest of the way, then grabbed for the snapping flag. It was large, but with a few hard tugs it tore free and floated to the ground, delighting the Americans. The halyard pulley was hung in place, and Van Arsdale came down. Immediately, the Stars and Stripes rose, and the artillery began to fire thirteen times in salute, once for each of the United States of America.

The British in their longboats, aboard the ships, and on Governor's Island could only look on in grudging respect. Perhaps some of them even recognized the voices of those cannon echoing across the water, for the guns firing the victorious salute to the American flag flying over liberated New York City included four six-pounders that had been captured from the British Army. As the guns fired, someone passed a hat so that John Van Arsdale could take more than just a remarkable story back to his bride. Even His Excellency, who for some time had been standing in the crowd watching it all, contributed with apparent pleasure.

FEASTING, FIREWORKS, EARTHQUAKES, AND WAITING

*I*N THE NEXT FEW DAYS THERE WERE dinners for Washington to attend and give, addresses of praise to receive and answer, foreign and American dignitaries to greet and to bid farewell, and a British fleet to observe in the harbor as it waited for a favorable wind and finished preparations for taking to sea.

Although the general wanted to be on his way home, he would not leave New York while that fleet hovered there, within a long musket shot of the city. No one expected any resumption of hostilities, but Washington was a man of principle, a man of his word. When the British set sail, he would go, too, but not before would his duty be complete.

That first evening in New York, Governor George Clinton gave a dinner in Washington's honor at Fraunces Tavern with more than one hundred and twenty guests. After the famed dessert concoctions of Sam Fraunces, there were thirteen joyous toasts, one for each independent state, and given in the following order:

1. "The United States of America."
2. "His most Christian Majesty." (King Louis XVI of France, whose alliance with the United States in 1778 tipped the balance against Britain.)
3. "The United Netherlands." (The Dutch also allied with America in the war and now were offering the new nation crucial loans.)

4. "The King of Sweden." (His merchant navy had defied British embargoes against the American colonies.)

5. "The American Army." (Surely the toast most heartfelt by everyone in the room.)

6. "The fleet and armies of France, which served in America." (In four years on the continent, the French army took part in one great victory, at Yorktown in 1781, and its fleet's signal success in American waters was a timely repulse of the British Navy during the same campaign.)

7. "The memory of those heroes who have fallen for our freedom."

8. "May our country be grateful to her military children." (Congress had a long way to go to show its gratitude; at least one of the officers at the dinner had been on a high-level delegation to persuade Congress to pay the troops' due, but he had returned empty-handed.)

9. "May justice support what courage has gained."

10. "The vindicators of the rights of mankind in every quarter of the globe."

11. "May America be an asylum to the persecuted of the earth."

12. "May a close union of the states guard the temple they have erected to liberty."

13. "May the remembrance of this day be a lesson to princes."

There was a brilliant display of fireworks that night, a thrilling firing-off of rockets, and bonfires were lit on many a corner, as the entire city was illuminated in honor of Evacuation Day.

The Fraunces Tavern Long Room, where Washington took leave of his officers.

*T*HE FOLLOWING DAY, NOVEMBER 26, WASHINGTON replied to the address of the "returning exiles"—one of several such answers to addresses and letters he would write in this time; others went to an Irish immigrant society, church and volunteer associations, and the New York Marine Society. He also wrote to Congress, which was waiting for him to come to Annapolis and hand over his commission.

Most of the replies to addresses were drafted by his longstanding aide-de-camp, Colonel David Humphreys, who well knew the general's thoughts and style in these matters.

> To the Citizens of New York who have returned from exile:
> Gentlemen: I thank you sincerely for your affectionate address, and entreat you to be persuaded that nothing could be more agreeable to me than your polite congratulations. Permit me, in turn, to felicitate you on the happy repossession of your city.... May the tranquility of your city be perpetual. May the ruins soon be repaired, commerce flourish, science be fostered; and all the civil and social virtues be cherished in the same illustrious manner which formerly reflected so much credit on the inhabitants of New York. In fine, may every species of felicity attend you gentlemen and your worthy fellow citizens.

While in New York, Washington did some shopping for clothing, household items for his wife, Martha, and he found toys that would especially please their grandchildren. Two years earlier the children had lost their father, Martha's natural son, whom Washington had adopted.

In this time, the general is said to have secretly visited espionage agents living in town. In an era when espionage was considered too dishonorable to admit to, the identities of most agents remained veiled long after the war. One of Washington's key spies—who perhaps switched sides solely out of crass opportunism, not patriotism—was said to be James Rivington, a well-known newspaper publisher whose *New York Gazette* had been the strident voice of loyalism throughout the war. One legend says Washington went to Rivington, whose print shop was a few blocks east of Fraunces Tavern, and gave the publisher a couple of bags of gold in payment for espionage services. Whatever Rivington was, he had made many dangerous enemies among the returning rebel exiles, and it would be virtually impossible to explain away his years of fierce public hostility to the cause of revolution.

Another alleged agent was Hercules Mulligan, whose tailor shop stood farther down the street from Rivington's offices. Washington went there to order a complete wardrobe, for after eight years in uniform, the general was in need of some civilian clothes. Mulligan, born in Ireland and a friend of Alexander Hamilton, Washington's former aide, was said to have picked up valuable military information from British officers who patronized his shop. He not only reported on troop arrivals and departures (deducing whether they were going to Canada or the South by the weight of new coats the officers ordered), but in at least one case also gave a timely warning that foiled an attempt to kidnap Washington. After the visit by His Excellency, Mulligan was entitled to the sign he soon hung by his door: "Clothier to Genl. Washington."

*T*HE CITY WAS A CONTINUOUS CELEBRATION, with much festivity in the streets late into the night. A song was written just for the occasion, entitled "The Sheep Stealers," mocking the British and their loyalist allies: the refugees and Tories.

> *King George sent his sheep-stealers,*
> *Poor refugees and Tories!*
> *King George sent his sheep-stealers*
>> *To fish for mutton here,*
>> *To fish for mutton here,*
>> *To fish for mutton here;*
> *But Yankees were hard dealers,*
>> *Poor refugees and Tories,*
> *But Yankees were hard dealers,*
>> *They sold their sheep-skins dear,*
>> *They sold their sheep-skins dear,*
>> *They sold their sheep-skins dear;*
> *But Yankees were hard dealers,*
>> *They sold their sheep-skins dear!*
>
> * * *
>
> *Of conquest then despairing,*
>> *With refugees and Tories,*
>> *George for his Bull-dogs sent;*
> *They Yankee vengeance fearing,*
>> *Greased the staff—and went!*

$\mathcal{O}$<small>N THE EVENING OF NOVEMBER</small> 26, Washington played host at a large dinner, this one also at Fraunces. Two days later, New York's leading citizens gave a banquet at Cape's Tavern in honor of Washington, Clinton, and the officers of the army. With more than three hundred in attendance, it was described as "an elegant entertainment."

The British fleet was yet in the bay.

On November 29, at about 10:30 p.m., the city shuddered to an earthquake tremor. There was an even stronger quake half an hour later, remembered by one startled New Yorker as "a severe shock…felt along the southern aspect [of the city] with the greatest force." It was a fitting token of change after the tumultuous years of the American Revolution.

On December 1, the merrymaking continued, as Governor Clinton gave another banquet at Cape's, this one in honor of the French ambassador, Chevalier de la Luzerne. There were three hundred guests, including Washington, who appeared quite weary, yet happy. The evening was full of good humor and laughter.

The next night, in celebration of the Treaty of Peace, Washington arranged an awe-inspiring fireworks display that delighted an enormous gathering of spectators in and around the city. He had originally intended to have the commemorative fireworks at the army's cantonment upriver in New Windsor, but the final peace terms had arrived too late, for the army was disbanding. Whenever the occasion warranted it during the war, Washington took great pleasure in holding colorful spectacles to mark special occasions. Sometimes he placed entire regiments on hillsides at night and had them fire their thousands of muskets in coordinated sequence—a rippling "fire of joy" flashing back and forth across the blackness.

This latest fireworks display, set in New York's Bowling Green, was an "unparalleled exhibition," the likes of which had never been seen in the city before. The celebration was all the more pleasing to Washington because the British had just reported they would sail with the afternoon tide on Thursday, December 4.

Broad Street, looking toward City Hall and Wall Street.

New York City in Revolutionary War days, showing Washington's procession through Queen Stret and Wall Street; Fort George is at left, and Frances Tavern is nearby.

Washington's Farewell

Thursday, December 4, 1783

No Ordinary Men

*T*ABLES AT ONE END OF FRAUNCES TAVERN'S Long Room were laid with a buffet luncheon for forty. Samuel Fraunces, his family, and staff worked diligently to make everything perfect for His Excellency's farewell to the remaining officers. Word had gone out to those few still in the city, inviting them to join the general here at the noon hour. They would appear soon, all of them knowing that after Washington departed for Annapolis, they probably would never see him again.

The room had a low ceiling and was well lit by tall, recessed windows facing Broad Street. Winter sunlight gleamed off the polished mahogany tables and reflected from looking glasses on the walls. China, crystal, and silverware were set on the tables alongside decanters of red wine and port next to pewter and silver tureens of hot and cold food. There were Delft blue punch bowls, plates of fruits and nuts, platters of cold meats, roasted and boiled, and an assortment of Fraunces's own pickled delicacies. All was prettily garnished with artificial flowers as decoration and centerpieces, some of them edible. There were desserts—cakes, tarts, jellies, whips, and sweetmeats—and the coffee was ready, cups stacked with saucers.

Sam Fraunces once said he always prepared his food "in as elegant a manner as lies in my power"; Washington had remarked that meals at Fraunces Tavern were in a "genteel style." Known for sitting long hours with guests at the dinner table, enjoying good conversation, good drink, and many courses—on occasion until suppertime—Washington appreciated Fraunces's artful cooking. The innkeeper was under stress these days, trying to recover from the war and long siege that had brought him to what he called the brink "of Beggary." The British had evacuated the city, but some officers had gone without paying their bills. With the return of peace, Fraunces hoped he would be able to reinvigorate his business, and Washington did what he could to help, hiring him to select such things as china and glassware to be sent back to Mount Vernon.

Competition among New York innkeepers was intense, but with the city still suffering from wartime shortages, few could offer more than the simplest fare. For Fraunces, having the favor of His Excellency and the victors meant there was the financial wherewithal to procure the very best that could be found. His hardworking household made the most of that. The staff usually consisted of fourteen persons, including himself and Elizabeth, his partner and wife; their two sons, five daughters, several indentured servants and slaves (also referred to as servants), a hired maid, and a waiter.

Proof of Washington's regard for Fraunces had been demonstrated a few weeks earlier when His Excellency asked him to come upriver to Dobb's Ferry and cater a conference with Sir Guy Carleton, commander of British forces in America. The meeting was to negotiate the evacuation of New York City. Sir Guy, a redcoat officer highly respected by Americans, had left the city just before Washington entered and was now aboard the warship *Ceres,* waiting for the tide to take his fleet out of the harbor.

The dinners Washington and Clinton gave in Fraunces Tavern in the happy days right after evacuation were further testimony of how high the innkeeper stood in their favor, not to mention how accomplished he was at his profession. This final gathering on December 4 was not a banquet, but Fraunces had everything in readiness to contribute to a most memorable occasion, including plenty of liquor and wine for toasts. It was a great honor to serve His Excellency on this sentiment-fraught occasion, and Fraunces had just written Washington to express regret that the general was leaving the city so soon.

The past days had been joyous for the war-weary city, but the celebration would end with the departure of the man who, more than any other, had brought about the victory. The history of New York City in the Revolution would also come to a close when Washington departed. A good deal of that history had played out here, in Fraunces Tavern, with its nine large rooms for elegant parties, five bedrooms with fireplaces, and a spacious and cozy ale room at street level. Throughout the war, the tavern's chambers often rang with laughter and song, no matter what the news or who was drinking, but its quieter corners were for intimate discussions, rumor, and sometimes conspiracy.

Fraunces Tavern was known as a charming public house for private clubs and companies of "Ladies and Gentlemen and others," but before the war those who gave it their custom included hard-edged rabble-rousers and plotters. The sipping of fine Madeira in one room was often accompanied by the quaffing of ale and grog in the next, all of it alternately spiced with spoken or unspoken curses on the Continental Congress or Parliament. It was at Fraunces Tavern, late in

1773, that the Sons of Liberty resolved to prevent the unloading of ships with British tea that bore a despised tax. Years later, during the redcoat occupation, alert patriots listened to the conversations of British officers who had imbibed too much and spoke too freely about what the army soon would do to the rebels.

When the British troops took over in late 1776, Fraunces and his family fled the city to New Jersey, but he had been captured in 1778 and forced to return to serve as steward for military governor Robertson during much of the war. From that position Fraunces heard much, and what information he could send to the rebels he did, in one deceptive way or another. He even saw to it that food went to sick and starving American captives lying in prisons, some of it coming right from the governor's leftovers.

For having stayed in New York throughout the occupation, Fraunces was more than once accused of being a loyalist sympathizer or at best an unpatriotic opportunist and friend to the British Army. In 1776, he was suspected of being a participant in a plot to assassinate Washington, but the general knew otherwise. Actually, Fraunces may have testified secretly in an investigation that overturned that very plot. When the war drew to a close, Washington publicly honored Fraunces as "a warm friend" and declared the innkeeper had "maintained a constant friendship and attention to the cause of our country and its independence and freedom."

In thanks for his efforts, financial reward eventually would be forthcoming to Sam Fraunces, from both the State of New York and the United States.

A British West Indian by birth, Samuel Fraunces came to New York City in the 1750s and was the proprietor of well-known inns patronized by redcoat and patriot alike; years after the war, Fraunces joined President Washington's household as his steward.

*D*APPER AND VIGOROUS, SAMUEL FRAUNCES was said to have been born around 1722, probably in the British West Indies. Of swarthy complexion, he was nicknamed "Black Sam"—not all that unusual for a white man; even Richard Lord Howe, a senior admiral of the British Navy, was nicknamed "Black Dick" because of his dark complexion.

Fraunces had come to New York in the early 1750s, at first known for his jars of condiments. By 1756 he had opened his own licensed tavern, offering a good meal any time of day, and advertising especially to sea travelers who could stock up on his fried and pickled oysters, lobsters, and beef, which would keep during long journeys. Successful, and earning a reputation as a chef as well as for his desserts and his good taste in Madeira wines, Fraunces bought the 1719 mansion built by the DeLanceys on the corner of Broad and Dock streets, near the bustling waterfront and the Exchange. The DeLanceys were the wealthiest and most powerful family of the city, most of them standing for the Tory cause, although offspring had intermarried with other leading families, some becoming rebels. The building, made of brick, had served as an office and warehouse before Fraunces bought it in 1762 for the considerable sum of two thousand pounds sterling. He hung out a sign with a portrait of Queen Charlotte, in homage to the wife of King George III, and the place became known as the Queen's Head.

In these years, Fraunces went on to open a "pleasure garden" in the upper west end of the city, calling it Vauxhall after the famous London public gardens. He leased his tavern on Broad and Dock to another operator while he managed

Vauxhall, where there was food and entertainment and a gallery of wax figures. Throughout much of the rebellion, Fraunces ran Vauxhall as well as his tavern, even while he was forced to steward for Governor Robertson.

As the noon hour approached, Fraunces's serving girls would have been hustling to place the final dishes, the waiter straightening silver and polishing tumblers, the servants removing trays and bringing in chairs. Fraunces himself would have overseen the last touches on the tables, so that all would be in readiness when the voices of guests were heard in the hall. He would have gone to welcome the guests by name, bowing low, and showing them into the Long Room as they arrived singly or in groups of three or four, most in full uniform, immaculate, boots polished, hair clubbed back and powdered white, here and there a black and white cockade worn on the lapel. Their coats and capes were blue, their smallclothes white or buff, while many of the turned-back facings were red in artillery regulation. Their hats were under their arms, capes left with servants at the front door. Some wore a fashionable frill at the cuff, taking the opportunity to be in a full dress uniform for once, instead of their more usual worn campaign clothes.

Crowding the room, glad to see each other again, shaking hands, bowing, exchanging the most courteous and formal greetings, or perhaps meeting with only a grin and a touch on the shoulder, they glittered today as seldom they had during the war. Their swords and canes were polished, and here and there gold or silver epaulets could be seen. Only a few generals and colonels were present, for most men of these ranks had retired and gone home—if they yet lived. An open invitation had gone out to all officers, and some in the Long

Room were only junior artillery lieutenants eager to see the great man up close. Every one was welcome. There were few enough as it was—not even forty in all—when so many others would have been grateful to be here and were missed.

They were few in number, but they were impressive, for these were not ordinary men. They were revolutionaries who, for a higher ideal of liberty, had risked all they held dear. Most had paid a high price, fighting on and on, but in the end they had overthrown a great empire, the mightiest military power of all. Today, they carried victory, and carried it like heroes, modestly, humbly. Washington was their example.

They carried, too, a profound memory of war, of hardship, defeat, and loss—of blood shed and lives lost in a cause that was no more, a cause transformed by triumph into a peacetime world they already did not know, that no one knew, for there had never been a time or a people or a revolution like this.

Reserved, almost hushed, they took glasses of wine or cider, picked on the buffet, and glanced frequently at the door in case His Excellency appeared. It had only been a few minutes, but the noon hour had come, and His Excellency was always prompt. Three or four of them would travel southward with Washington, and several would continue with the army for as long as necessary, but most were returning to private life after eight difficult years under arms. This would be their last scene as revolutionary soldiers before the curtain of peace closed on the stage—a stage that had been so much easier to understand than that which awaited when they left this room. They would begin again, but they would never forget.

This farewell would be the sealing of a bond with the man they called the father of the country they had made with him, by their own hands, and with so much sacrifice.

THE INCENDIARY

*S*OME OF THESE OFFICERS KNEW FRAUNCES TAVERN and Black Sam well, but none better than Colonel John Lamb, whose family home was around the corner on Wall Street. Or what was left of it, after years of soldiers or loyalists living there.

In his late forties, Lamb had twenty years ago been one of the first opponents of Parliament's colonial policy and one of the first Sons of Liberty. With his friends Alexander McDougall, Alexander Hamilton, and Isaac Sears, he had planned and carried out opposition to the British government's policies, had written and published handbills that chastised the governor and Parliament. As early as the 1760s, when the British Parliament was laying down oppressive regulations and tariffs in order to raise taxes in America and stem colonial aspirations for self-rule, Lamb had formed associations to unite with like-thinkers in other colonies. He had protested the Stamp Act of 1765, stood shoulder-to-shoulder with those who burned the colonial governor's gilded coach (with an effigy of the governor inside) on New York's Bowling Green, and helped raise, and raise again, liberty poles that were periodically chopped down by the redcoat garrison. He had been a member of New York's Provincial Congress, established in opposition to the conservative Provincial Assembly that was all too pliable when it came to the wishes of Parliament across the sea in England.

By profession a wine merchant and engraver, Lamb had become a friend of Boston's Paul Revere, also an engraver. Late in 1773, when Boston gave its momentous "tea party," Lamb had put up Revere, who was riding through with the news to the Continental Congress in Philadelphia. In the spring of 1774, Lamb was behind the plot to throw taxed tea into New York harbor, planning the move here in Fraunces Tavern. From early acts of resistance to open rebellion and warfare, Lamb had been at the forefront of it all, and now here he was at the very end. His service to the cause had cost him a badly scarred face, the result of surprise enemy artillery fire in a blinding snowstorm during the failed American assault on Quebec City in the winter of 1775-76.

*T*HE WINE MERCHANT AND ENGRAVER had become an accomplished artillerist for the cause of revolution. Late in the summer of 1775, after the opening of hostilities, the Provincial Congress had called for new forts to be built and armed to guard Hudson's River against the "army of Parliament," and this required guns. The most readily available, twenty-one of them, were on the battery of unmanned Fort George, which the British had abandoned in order to reinforce Boston, where they were under siege by colonial militias led by George Washington.

The fighting had begun in New England, with no turning back. New York City was a strategic key to control of the colonies, so it was only a matter of time before the British Navy appeared in force to land thousands of soldiers and occupy the city. For months, the towering battleship HMS

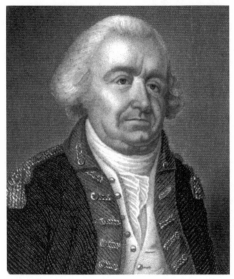

An early member of the New York Sons of Liberty and an artillery-man for Washington, John Lamb was a prime mover in the city's anti-British demonstrations.

Asia with its sixty-two guns had dominated and overshad-owed New York from its anchorage in the East River. At a word, the *Asia* could batter the city to ruins in a matter of hours, wreaking widespread destruction and death. Week after week, month after month, the people of the city—whether for or against Parliament or the revolutionaries—lived in uncertainty, dreading the opening of hostilities that could wipe out their city.

Yet insurgents like Lamb and his friends, with the help of Sons of Liberty from Connecticut, had deliberately defied the *Asia* and taunted its captain. A sloop belonging to the warship had been boarded by radicals, its crew briefly arrested, and the vessel burned. Even the anti-Parliament New York Provincial Congress stopped short of condoning such reck-lessness, especially when the weight of so much naval artillery could be brought to bear in revenge. It ordered a replacement sloop built as restitution; but before long the radicals struck again, sawing the new boat to pieces and threatening the shipwrights if they ever tried to make another.

This was followed by the raid on Fort George on the night of August 23, a raid that had not been kept secret enough, for the captain of the *Asia* had been warned. Lamb and his comrades, including young Alexander Hamilton and his friend the tailor Hercules Mulligan, entered the fort at midnight and began to dismantle and haul the artillery away. Working in the dim light of masked lanterns and with much banging and clattering of tools and rumbling of wheels on cobblestones, the insurgents moved guns up Broadway toward the city Commons, a few blocks away. An artillery piece could weigh as much as two thousand pounds, and most had only small wheels, so a dozen men were needed to haul a single gun. As their comrades sweated away, a line of sentries armed with muskets stood facing the water, where trouble might appear.

It did not take long for Lamb and Hamilton to spot a British sloop, its sail down, drifting in the darkness. The *Asia* had sent this boat, loaded with armed men, to observe what was going on at the fort. The American sentries, among them Hamilton and Mulligan, anxiously looked to their muskets, expecting an attack at any moment. The slow work dismantling the guns proceeded, and nothing happened on either the sloop or the *Asia*.

Then, after eight or ten guns had been moved, a single musket fired from the sloop. Perhaps the shot had been a signal to the *Asia,* or was just the accidental triggering of a firelock by a sleepy sailor. Whatever happened, on this night New York City heard the first gunfire of the Revolution. The

A contemporary view of New York from the northwest, with Fort George at right.

nervous sentries guarding the work parties removing the artillery turned their muskets on the boat and flashed a volley. The sloop's men returned the fire, but they were outgunned and withdrew out of range, a sailor shot dead.

The work continued until the *Asia* fired a cannon at the fort, the flash lighting up the harbor, the boom pealing across the rooftops as the cannonball crashed into a rampart. The sleeping city was jarred awake. The dismantling came to a temporary halt. New York's radicals had sent all their black powder to the militia besieging Boston, so there was no way to reply to the *Asia*. Just as well, for amateur artillerymen would have been helpless against skilled naval gunners. A moment later, another cannon fired from the *Asia,* and this time grapeshot spattered over Fort George's ramparts and battery. In the darkness, it was hard to tell whether anyone had been hurt, but Lamb's men kept on with their work. A second blast of grapeshot came whizzing and ricocheting their way, and then another. Now the work stopped, as the men took cover.

Some time passed. The *Asia* had stopped firing. The insurgents discussed what to do next. The entire city was awake, lamps in windows, lanterns carried outdoors by people who feared their nightmares had come true: If the *Asia* let go with a sustained barrage, the city was doomed. Terrified folk swarmed through the streets lugging hastily gathered belongings and headed north up York Island or to the ferries that would take them across Hudson's River or the East River, anywhere, just to get away from impending disaster. The insurgents went back to work on the guns, despite the *Asia*'s warning. They had come too far to stop now.

The laborious, slow work of dismantling the artillery and dragging each gun away to the Commons went on until three in the morning, when the night erupted with a thunderous blast of thirty-two naval guns, an entire broadside from the *Asia*. Though aimed at Fort George, iron shot caromed and bounced wherever it would, crashing into walls and rooftops, garden gates, and chimneys. The city shook, windows cracked, people shrieked and prayed and took cover. It was an unforgettable moment, a foretaste of imminent doom. Lamb's raiders melted away into the city to wait for their next opportunity.

For all the shock and terror, only three or four citizens had been injured by the broadside, and there was no bombardment. The *Asia* intended a warning to New York, not devastation. She did not fire again, and the stolen artillery got no farther than the city Commons, where it lay untouched for weeks. The royal governor wanted to restore peace, so he promised no retribution to the troublemakers and no more broadsides from the *Asia*, as long as the guns were left alone.

A cannonball from the barrage had crashed through the roof of Sam Fraunces's tavern. When New York returned to calm a day or two later, the hole in the roof of the Queen's Head was an object of curiosity. Likely it was good for business, especially from Lamb's and Hamilton's faction, already regular customers. That would help pay Sam's repair bill.

Contemporary poet Philip Freneau later memorialized the terrible moment when a British warship actually fired on a British city. In the poem he referred to Fraunces as Francis, and mentioned two well-known smaller vessels of the time—the tea ship *Nancy*, boarded by the New York Sons of Liberty, who jettisoned its cargo, and the *Sally*, a sloop belonging to Benedict Arnold before the war. For dramatic effect, Freneau exaggerated the number of broadsides fired by the *Asia*.

Scarce a broadside was ended 'till another began again.
  By Jove! it was nothing but Fire Away Flannagan!
Some thought him saluting his Sally's *and* Nancy's
  'Till he drove a round shot through the roof of Sam Francis.

In another verse:

At first we supposed it was only a sham,
  'Till he drove a round ball through the roof of Black Sam.

One day those guns from the Fort George battery would be remounted to defend New York City; but first they would be scattered around the region, captured and lost, recaptured, spiked, and repaired. Rather than John Lamb—who would spend the rest of 1775 and much of the next year invading Canada and then as a British captive—it would be another artillery commander who would make the next use of New York City's guns: Henry Knox of Boston.

KNOX AND TICONDEROGA'S GUNS

*S*TANDING WITH THE OFFICERS IN FRAUNCES'S Long Room, Major-general Henry Knox was the most prominent figure, in part because of his massive physical size—a giant next to the slim, boyish Alexander Hamilton—but mainly for his future as the next commander-in-chief of the American Army.

In a few days, Washington's resignation would open the

way for Knox to take full charge of the peacetime military establishment. For all the honor coming his way, there was no man more sorry to see Washington leave, no man who held His Excellency in higher regard, no officer who had been more dependable and effective than Henry Knox.

Like John Lamb, Knox had been working for American rights well before April 19, 1775, when the fighting began at Lexington and Concord. Also like Lamb he had been a marked man, with the British Army and loyalists following his movements while he trained as a lieutenant with his militia company in Boston. When unrest became a crisis that spring of 1775, Knox was forbidden to leave the city without a pass from the authorities. Yet he could not be prevented from studying military tactics, strategy, and drilling, which he learned from the books he sold in his Boston book shop. He had then been in his mid-twenties, active and strong in spite of being overweight, with a mind hungry for the knowledge found in military books he ordered from England.

Along with the popular fiction on his shelves were treatises on the art of war by European luminaries. The texts that most appealed to Knox were those on army engineering and artillery. Perhaps nowhere else in America could a better collection of books on military matters be found. Just offering these books to potential rebels was an act of defiance, and when men such as Rhode Island's Nathanael Greene visited Knox's book shop, it was likely that much of their talk was of military history, maneuvers, and engineering. Knox's patrons included Henry Jackson of Massachusetts, who was also waiting in Fraunces Tavern for Washington to arrive, and the Massachusetts activists Sam Adams, James Otis, and Paul Revere. Surely New York's John Lamb and Alexander

Commander of the Continental artillery, Henry Knox, a Bostonian, was with Washington's army throughout the war and later succeeded him as commander-in-chief.

Hamilton had an interest in Knox's military collection, too, and when Hamilton visited the city soon after the Boston Tea Party, a visit to the bookseller would have put hard-to-find artillery manuals in his hands.

When news of the bloody clashes at Lexington and Concord electrified Boston, Knox knew he had to get out of the city immediately, before he was arrested by the army. After dark, he and his wife, Lucy, cautiously drove their carriage through the winding, narrow streets, which were crowded with hurrying folk. Thousands of people were on the move, including radicals leaving the city to join their kind, and loyalists entering for protection. Wounded and dying redcoats were everywhere, their blood running in the gutters as they lay on pallets awaiting medical help or for friends and family to find them. How Knox escaped was partly a matter of luck, and partly because of the chaos reigning in Boston that night, for he was well known, as was his wife. Lucy's family was staunchly loyal, her only brother an officer in the British Army. Had they been stopped, however, no cursory search would have uncovered Henry's militia sword, which Lucy had sewn into her petticoats.

Within days, Knox had offered the rebel army that sword, as well as his self-taught knowledge of military engineering and gunnery. Henry and Lucy Knox abandoned their families, home, and business for the rebellion. His skills were to be employed by the rebels to attack his own city, where many friends and Lucy's parents were under siege by an American militia army.

*T*HE PROVINCIAL CONGRESS OF Massachusetts sent a letter to committees of safety, as local rebel leaders were named: "Gentlemen—The barbarous Murders of our innocent Brethren…[have] made it absolutely necessary that we immediately raise an army to defend our Wives and our Children from the butchering Hands of an inhuman soldiery, who will, without the least doubt, take the first Opportunity to ravage this devoted Country with Fire and Sword."

The appeal by the Massachusetts Provincial Congress was answered not only by its own people, but by the Continental Congress convening then in Philadelphia to unite the colonies in common cause against Parliament. The outbreak in Massachusetts ignited a war spirit and the movement to establish a Continental Army. On June 15, George Washington, colonel of the Virginia militia, was chosen as commander-in-chief. John Adams, a delegate from Massachusetts, proposed Washington, commending the Virginian's "skill and experience as an officer, whose independent fortune, great talents, and excellent universal character would command the approbation of all America, and unite the cordial exertions of all the colonies better than any other person in the Union."

In acceptance, Washington replied with typical modesty: "Though I am truly sensible of the high honor done me on this appointment, yet I feel great distress from a consciousness that my abilities and military experience may not be equal to the extensive and important trust. However, as Congress desires I will enter upon the momentous duty and exert every power I possess in their service for the support of the glorious cause.... I beg it may be remembered by every gentleman in the room, that I this day declare with the utmost sincerity, I do not think myself equal to the command I am honored with."

Others of those gentlemen in Congress were eager for this same position and resented Washington's getting it. Had they received the appointment, their acceptances likely would not have been so modest. In the years to come, whether in defeat or victory, jealous men would make trouble for General Washington.

A FEW WEEKS LATER, SHORTLY after the June 17 Battle of Bunker Hill, Washington was in the sprawling rebel camp, with headquarters at Cambridge. What met him there was troubling to a general who needed discipline and efficiency.

The army was in no way an organized military force capable of maneuvering in the open field or of standing up against British regulars except from behind strong earthworks. Instead, on Washington's hands were thousands of enthusiastic but utterly undisciplined volunteers, a mass of carousing, fighting, hungry, British-hating New Englanders who were too democratic to obey orders, and were suspicious of a stranger from distant Virginia showing up to tell them what to do.

"I found a mixed multitude of people here, under very little discipline, order, or government," Washington wrote home to his brother. His first labors were to throw up new defensive works to prevent the British from breaking out of the city.

As for the force at his command, he wrote to fellow Continental general Philip Schuyler of Albany: "confusion and disorder reign in every department." He later called the New England officers "indifferent," some of them corrupt and cowardly. He believed the "Men would fight very well (if properly officered)," but one of his first unsavory duties was to court-martial officers accused of cowardice at Bunker Hill—the battle that most Yankee rebels considered a point of pride. Many resented this southerner's heavy hand coming down on them. After all, they had left the comforts of home and hearth to be here.

The militia besieging Boston had been away from farm and family for more than two months, and by the time Washington showed up, many considered their duty already done and were about to leave. Others had enlisted for a longer term, but that would be up by wintertime. Most had farms and families that desperately needed their hands just then. Many had been in the thick of the first battles, but their new general was untested except for his participation in some middling successes and notable defeats twenty years earlier, during the French and Indian War.

That August, the general wrote to a Virginia congressional delegate: "There has been so many great and capital errors and abuses to rectify—so many examples to make—and so little inclination in the officers of inferior rank to contribute their aid to accomplish the work, that my life has been nothing else (since I came here) but one continued round of annoyance...." He added that no amount of money could have persuaded him to accept this task of disciplining an insolent army of men who listened only to their own officers. In demanding military decorum he rendered himself "very obnoxious to a greater part of these People."

Word of his complaints about New Englanders riled the congressmen from the region, including John Adams, who bridled to hear that Washington considered many of the Massachusetts troops dirty as well as money-grubbing:

Washington reviewing troops at Cambridge, Massachusetts.

"there is no nation under the sun ... that pay greater adoration to money than they do." The general wrote to a Virginia delegate that New Englanders were even unwilling to be vigilant against British attack: "It is among the most difficult tasks I ever undertook in my life to induce these people to believe that there is, or can be, danger till the bayonet is pushed at their breasts." He also complained that the Massachusetts officers were too inclined to "curry favor with the men (by whom they were chosen, and upon whose smiles they may think they may again rely)...."

Hearing about Washington's attitude, and faced with his urgent demands for supplies and cash for the army, Adams began to wonder whether the general was too much the patrician planter to understand New Englanders. Then came rumors that he favored men from the South over northerners—even though he had decisively and forcefully put down and punished a mutiny of Virginia riflemen who had threatened their officers for arresting one of their own.

Washington had raw power before him, almost twenty thousand men at one point, but he needed good officers, and that meant disciplining the bad ones, breaking the worst to lower rank. The sort of leaders he needed were recognizable by the condition of their units' encampments, by the discipline of the men under their command. The best officers were beacons in the darkness, shining examples amid the slovenliness and insolence of officers who did not understand that final victory would take an organized military, well-led and resolute, obedient, willing to sacrifice for many months, perhaps even years, to come. One of the first men Washington took note of was Nathanael Greene and his Rhode Islanders. Another was Henry Jackson of Massachusetts.

One of the most remarkable was Henry Knox, who was in turn impressed by the general. Washington was taking hold of the army with an ever-tightening grip, and Knox admired him for that. The aspiring young officer wrote to his brother: "General Washington fills his place with vast ease and dignity, and dispenses happiness around him."

From the start, Washington noticed the well-designed and constructed forts at Roxbury, which Knox and another officer had built. It was thought that no capable military engineer was available to the American rebels, but after years of serving alongside British Army engineers, Washington recognized that Knox had the makings of a good one. "A very fat but active young man," was how the general described him, adding that he had "a jubilant personality." Not only was Knox a fast-learning army engineer, but he knew about artillery, another essential skill in short supply in Washington's army—although not as scarce as guns themselves.

It would require heavy artillery bearing on Boston and the naval shipping in the harbor to force the British under military governor General Thomas Gage to evacuate. Washington's army had little artillery, but Knox's guns were well placed and served by good men. Before long, the former bookseller was promoted to colonel and overall commander of the regiment of artillery. Already, he was formulating an ambitious plan to acquire all the artillery needed to bombard the city of Boston, his own home.

*T*HROUGHOUT THE LAST LONG AND wearying months of 1775, Washington had improved his army in ways that the unmilitary minds and financial committees of the Continental Congress at Philadelphia—including John Adams—did not understand. What the politicians wanted was action, immediate attack. Washington's army seemed enormous, and it was distressingly expensive to feed and keep in camp. Warm weather was for campaigning, but Washington appeared to be doing nothing. Was he so indecisive? Did he really have no faith in New Englanders, who made up the bulk of the force?

Never mind that his headquarters staff was increasingly able and devoted to him for the most part, or that Henry Knox had developed an artillery regiment, or that the men were drilling regularly and learning the manual of arms. Also, absences without leave had been reduced, the rash of soldiers plundering private homes curtailed. The general had proven that punishment for offenses would be harsh and swift, whether by the lash or by drumming out. He had also begun to instill a sense of pride in being a good American soldier engaged in a noble cause that was even higher than a man's allegiance to his state.

By autumn, all Congress cared about was that the British garrison numbered five thousand regulars fit for duty while Washington had more than sixteen thousand soldiers. In fact, there were also five thousand loyalist fighting men available to the enemy, and the entire city was heavily fortified against attack. Enemy defenses were so strong that Washington believed a thousand resolute men could repel twenty thousand attackers. Moreover, many in the rebel army had no weapons, with no prospects that Congress would raise the funds to provide them—not firelocks, tents, or gunpowder, nor the hard money to pay troops, buy supplies, hire wagons and draft animals, and sustain the myriad day-to-day operations. There was much more to generalship than attacking, but Congress did not want to hear that. They grumbled that a good commander made do with what he had.

Washington intended to avoid a large-scale engagement if possible, and force Gage out by a dull but deadly siege. An open battle would favor the enemy regulars. It troubled Washington to hear Congress declare this was "the season for action," yet fail to furnish the means. Above all else, he needed more artillery mounted across the bay from Boston. Heavy guns would be far more of a threat than twice his force of inexperienced militia could ever be. Washington was intrigued when Henry Knox proposed taking the artillery from far-off forts Ticonderoga and Crown Point on Lake Champlain, which had been captured last spring by Green Mountain militia led by Ethan Allen and Benedict Arnold. This winter, with the rivers, lakes, and roads frozen and covered with snow, the guns could be sledded all the way to Boston.

Washington approved the plan, though it would be a grueling, uncertain journey through wilderness and mountains, at risk of blizzards and bitter cold that could kill men and animals in their tracks.

*I*N NOVEMBER OF 1775 KNOX began his expedition to get the Fort Ticonderoga artillery. First he rode overland to New York City, with Washington's orders to arrange for essential artillery supplies and ammunition to be forwarded to Boston in time for the arrival of the guns. In New York, Knox had an eye on those artillery pieces from Fort George, but they were needed for the defense of the city, so he was not permitted to requisition them.

From there, he journeyed up the valley of Hudson's River to Albany, and after consulting with General Philip Schuyler, who lent his local influence to help him in many ways, Knox traveled to Ticonderoga. On a ferociously cold day early in December, the trek to Boston began. It would be an expedition of more than two hundred and fifty miles, with some water passage but mostly over frozen trails. At least fifty-nine pieces were to be hauled, ranging from brass field guns to heavy mortars and huge howitzers.

The artillery alone—some guns weighing a hundred pounds and others fifty-five hundred pounds—totaled 119,000 pounds. Also carried were gun flints, and boxes of lead for making projectiles. It was an undertaking fit only for inspired young men. Indeed, Knox's youthful inexperience and ignorance of the coming ordeal might have been a blessing, considering what his expedition would have to endure before it was done. He would have to hire and manage additional teamsters, equipment, and animals, paying with promissory notes drawn on Congress. Sometimes he would have to persuade a local farmer to rent himself and a team for short, especially steep distances. There were constant mishaps, requiring repair or replacement of equipment. At one point early in the journey a scow laden with cannon ran aground and had to be laboriously dragged free. Soon afterward it swamped and sank, fortunately close to shore. Knox exercised his mighty strength of will to get it raised again, bailed out, and put back on course.

The expedition had to avoid taking a wrong turn that might lead to impassable terrain and force them to retrace their steps. Through it all, Knox kept up the spirits of his men, saw that they were fed and sheltered, healthy and sober, as they braved "roads that never bore a cannon before and never have borne one since," according to his brother William, who participated. Much of the region was sparsely populated, still haunted by the memory of savage raids and counterraids with the French and Indians. Images of this new war were also to be seen: closely guarded supply depots and new forts near Albany; mounted patrols riding back and forth on the roads; movement of fresh troops toward Canada, as well as battle casualties on their way homeward. There were British prisoners under guard, men who had been captured in the American invasion of Quebec, where John Lamb and Benedict Arnold were fighting and falling wounded.

One of the British prisoners was debonair young Lieutenant John Andre, taken that autumn in the first American push against Canada. Now on his way to Pennsylvania, eventually to be released on parole, Andre was a companionable roommate for Knox while they shared a room and a bed at Fort George, on the southern tip of Lake George. They were about the same age, with a shared passion for literature and the military, both accomplished young men on a swift rise to prominence in their respective armies.

Perhaps inspired by his encounter with Lieutenant Andre, who wrote about his war experiences, Knox began from this time forward to keep a diary.

The colonel had plenty to record. More than once, while the expedition was crossing streams or lakes, guns fell through the ice, and it could take all of a day, with the help of local people, to drag them out again. Knox would not leave one cannon behind, if he could at all help it. Near Albany, he had holes cut through the ice of Hudson's River to permit water to flood over the surface and then freeze to a stronger thickness, so that the caravan could safely cross. It required great energy and ingenuity to haul guns over mountains, and almost as much to keep them from sliding out of control when going down the other side. On they went, to the sounds of whips cracking, oxen lowing, teamsters cursing and snarling, as the long caravan of artillery climbed away from the Hudson Valley, through the narrow passes of the Taconic Range, and into the Berkshire hills.

Knox admired the lovely panoramas of mountain and sky, but wrote in his diary that it seemed "almost a miracle that people with heavy loads should be able to get up and down such hills as are here." Yet no one had a heavier load than he, relentlessly hacking and hauling his way along the sides of mountains, sometimes skirting swampy areas on terrain that was fine for normal passage of wagons and horsemen but which would never hold a cannon, let alone a train of fifty-nine of them. Many a local wondered how Knox did it, and in at least one case it was remarked that there had never been any kind of road where he was forging his way through. At one point, Knox had to defuse a near-mutiny, persuading a group of dispirited men not to turn back, but to persevere just a little longer, when they would come to easier country.

Before Knox's expedition was clear of the mountains, John Lamb, Ethan Allen, and three hundred men had been taken prisoner by the British, the Canada invasion a failure. All this while, men in Washington's army at Boston were going home in droves, their enlistments up. Few were willing even to hear out their general's arguments for staying. They had better things to do than sit and stare at the British locked in the city. More than ever, Washington had to move against Gage before the army eroded to nothing. More than ever, he needed Knox to bring those guns from Ticonderoga.

He got them by the end of January.

To General Washington's great joy, a "noble train of artillery" was at last under his command, along with a solid regiment of artillerymen led by a colonel who would never let him down. Of all Washington's generals, the majority of whom were fine commanders, Knox was outstanding as one of the most resourceful and effective.

On March 2, 1776, Washington fired the guns at Boston.

The bombardment began at midnight, and was watched with mixed feelings by the New England men in the rebel army. Knox himself feared for his in-laws, his home, and book shop. Another officer, Lieutenant Samuel Webb of Connecticut, who would later be waiting with Knox in Fraunces Tavern, wrote: "From my window, [I] have a most pleasing and yet dismal view of the fiery ministers of death flying through the air. Poor inhabitants, our friends, we pity most sincerely, but particularly the women and children."

The firing at Boston went on for three successive nights, shell after shell arcing through the sky to explode in the city, until the British and loyalists evacuated by sea. The anxious

Washington rode out on a peninsula to watch the last sails of the fleet disappear over the horizon. He wanted to make sure the departure was not a ruse, and that the enemy would not land their troops again and attack.

*T*HE VERY SAME THOUGHT COULD have been worrying His Excellency seven and a half years later, on December 4, 1783, as the British fleet hovered in New York Bay.

Washington had no army with which to oppose the British if suddenly they disembarked those six thousand troops to renew the war. Nor was there a noble train of artillery to engage the hundreds of guns on the warships serenely waiting for the tide and wind. The British fleet in the harbor was about to leave—everyone in Fraunces Tavern was certain of that—but His Excellency had scheduled his own departure from New York to coincide precisely with the afternoon tide. When the British and Sir Guy Carleton raised anchor, then and not before would Washington consider his duty as commander-in-chief complete.

His duty as an American, however, as patriot and republican, would not be complete until he handed over his commission to Congress, proving by this solemn deed that a virtuous military man would always subordinate himself to the elected government. There had been occasions when the men now in the Long Room had disagreed with that idea. There had been a time when they wanted him to lead them in armed threat against a Congress that had used, scorned, and betrayed them.

*I*N THOSE DARK DAYS OF NEAR MUTINY against Congress, even General Alexander McDougall, indomitable patriot, Son of Liberty, and foremost mentor of New York radicals, might have marched on Congress alongside Washington. If Washington had led them, as so many officers wished, then even McDougall—champion of civil liberty, the first prominent American radical to be imprisoned for writings and speeches hostile to the tyranny of taxation without representation—even he likely would have touched his sword hilt in threat.

McDougall could not have denied the precarious, crumbling edge he would have walked, risking all he had fought for since 1765. If it came to a coup, he would have known the danger of unleashing a new tyranny of armed force, of a terrible new war—this one even more a civil war than the Revolution. Other than Washington, McDougall—commander of the 1st New York—was as respected as any man in a rebel uniform, and he might very well have been the one asked to lead the officers against Congress. But Washington had stood as an immovable bulwark in the storm of controversy and mutiny, which had passed because he begged it to.

McDougall well knew how to lead, although one of his finest moments had been during a perilous retreat, when he had to shepherd the army out of defeat. That defeat had occurred on Long Island in 1776, and the escape had been from the Brooklyn ferry landing across the East River, to near this spot on lower York Island. If that escape had failed, if McDougall had not been equal to organizing it all, the army and the Revolution would have been lost.

A MIRACULOUS ESCAPE

*I*T RAINED HARD ON THE NIGHT of August 29, 1776, an unseasonably cold and dreary downpour that swept over western Long Island and chilled the drenched rebel army to the bone. It was a blessing.

The American army of nine thousand five hundred men lay trapped behind hastily thrown-up earthworks, pinned against the East River by more than twenty-five thousand confident British and German troops led by General William Howe. For three days the Americans had reeled from swift, battering attacks that had turned their left, enveloped their right, captured two generals, and wiped out whole battalions of stubborn fighting men who often were given no quarter by the enemy.

Washington had helplessly watched his army cut to pieces, and as he saw so many of them go down fighting courageously, he lamented, "Good God! What brave fellows I must this day lose."

Valiant Maryland and Delaware battalions had been destroyed, but only after fearlessly counterattacking, charging overwhelming odds. Outflanked, the American army had retreated to last-ditch positions near the Brooklyn ferry landing and turned to meet the decisive enemy assault. The rebels were crammed into two square miles of land, their backs to the mile-wide river, their defensive works inadequate, though they tried to dig in before the rain deluged them. The soldiers, many of them little older than boys, were exhausted, shaken, hungry, and cold; they were soaked to the skin by the chilling rainstorm and harried by lightning. Some fellows in McDougall's own 1st New York Regiment had been killed by a bolt that burned them to cinders in their trench.

That rain was fortuitous, slowing the enemy advance, giving the Americans time and Washington the opportunity to save what he could. It also gave General Howe an excuse for not making a frontal attack on the shattered Americans. Howe had been at Bunker Hill the previous year, had led the assaults that cost half the attacking force before the rebels withdrew. He had good reason to hesitate before launching another reckless frontal attack.

Washington took what he was given. At a council of war in a stone Dutch church, he called on Alexander McDougall, who had been a sea captain and a privateer in the last war with France, to supervise the embarkation of the entire army in one night. The men had to be transported to York Island before dawn, when the British in their trenches a couple of hundred yards away would surely see the Americans abandoning their works. Every man knew that if the enemy discovered the attempted escape, redcoats and Hessians would come pouring in, brandishing bayonets, and they were not in the mood to take prisoners.

McDougall, who had a slight speech impediment, told the council of war that if all went perfectly the army could be carried across the water to safety. The maneuver required absolute quiet, for while the British might have trouble seeing through the darkness and rain, they could hear if a soldier sneezed in the American camp. There was little room for error.

Washington's most intrepid spy master, handling secret relations with agents in enemy-held territory in and around New York, Benjamin Tallmadge, from Connecticut, was an excellent dragoon officer who served throughout the war.

Massachusetts fishermen from Salem, Gloucester, and Marblehead reverted to their profession as boatmen, and they took charge of whatever could float. Every vessel was ordered across to the Brooklyn ferry from York Island, to be loaded in semi-darkness, with the only light coming from masked lanterns. Front-line troops were shifted, regiment by regiment, back to the ferry landing for embarkation. To disguise this gradual retrograde movement and prevent the slightest hint of what was being done, Washington spread the false rumor among his troops and in New York City that the boats were being commandeered to fetch more regiments from New Jersey. Even many rebel officers were not informed of precisely what was happening, lest the word reach soldiers on picket, who might be captured by an enemy raiding party and forced to talk. (For similar reasons, Washington

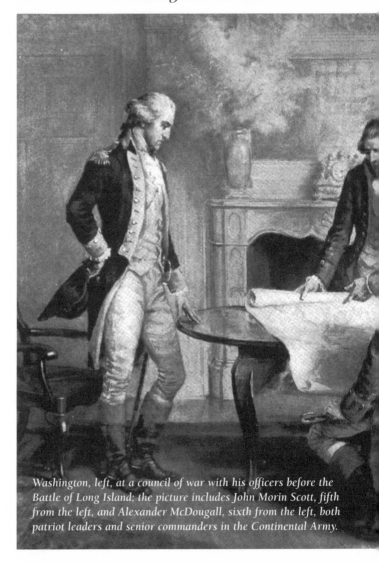

Washington, left, at a council of war with his officers before the Battle of Long Island; the picture includes John Morin Scott, fifth from the left, and Alexander McDougall, sixth from the left, both patriot leaders and senior commanders in the Continental Army.

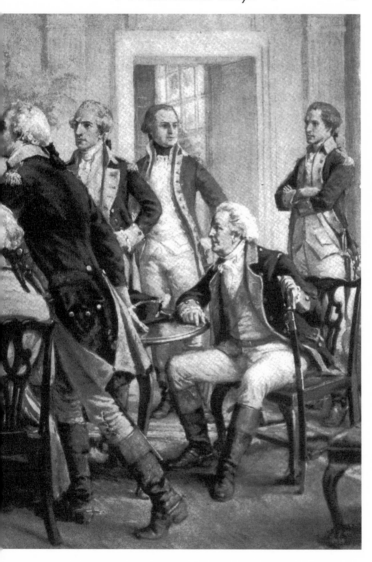

throughout the war kept his plans to himself and a few close, trusted subordinates, which sometimes caused other officers to think he had no plans, or that he played favorites.)

The embattled Americans on Long Island believed they were being called away from their front-line positions to be replaced by fresh troops. Meanwhile, units remaining in the lines were told to spread out to the right and left, to take the places of those that pulled out. Campfires were stoked up to give the illusion of activity in the rebel lines. As the withdrawal proceeded, silent columns of bedraggled, weary men trudged through the mud down to the ferry docks. Unsuspecting, they were surprised to find themselves ordered on board boats and taken out on the water, leaving the island.

Hundreds, then thousands, were on the move, with artillery, baggage, supplies, and horses as well. McDougall saw to it that men and materiel were shipped off with utmost efficiency, as all the while he listened for gunfire alerting him that the British had discovered the withdrawal and were attacking. Boats of all shapes and sizes, under sail or oar, crowded the ferry slips. Sometimes they appeared unexpectedly out of the darkness, colliding with others, but nerves and tempers were kept under control, and every man remained hushed as he worked—and as the army slowly escaped.

Throughout the night, Washington rode back and forth on his charger, appearing here, then in the next moment somewhere else, encouraging the men, exhorting them to have faith, instilling steadiness and courage by his own example. Then came a startling explosion that echoed in the night. He galloped off to find a loaded cannon had fired by accident. The army was breathless. Would the blast bring the enemy to investigate? After waiting, listening, Washington could sigh with relief that Howe's slumbering army had been untroubled by the sound.

When Colonel Edward Hand, commander of a dependable Pennsylvania regiment, appeared at the head of his men, ready to be embarked, Washington was stunned to see them. Hand's troops were supposed to be among the very last out of the forward defenses. If the Pennsylvanians were here at the docks while thousands of other soldiers were still waiting for boats, then there was a huge gap in the front line.

"It is a dreadful mistake!" Washington exclaimed, knowing something had gone wrong in the chain of command.

Without hesitation, Hand led his men back to their original position in a central redoubt. There in the darkness they settled down, saw to their priming, and waited. If the enemy discovered the embarkation of the army before the escape was complete, the Pennsylvanians would be overrun, and they knew it. Resolutely, they stayed. They would fight before they would run. That was why Washington had chosen them for this duty.

Long before dawn, the rain stopped, but it was colder than ever.

$\mathcal{T}$HROUGHOUT THAT NERVE-WRACKING NIGHT of Washington's deepest crisis thus far, young Connecticut dragoon officer Benjamin Tallmadge labored to help get men and equipment down to the ferry slip and onto boats.

Tallmadge wondered how Washington could "move so large a body of troops, with all their necessary appendages, across a river a full mile wide, with a rapid current, in the face of a victorious, well-disciplined army nearly three times as numerous as his own, and a [British] fleet capable of stopping the navigation so that not one boat could have passed over...."

Indeed, the enemy fleet would strike swiftly if boats were still on the water at dawn.

Tallmadge was utterly exhausted, still smarting from defeat in the first battle of his life. It was one of the "most anxious, busy nights that ever I recollect, and being the third in which hardly any of us had closed our eyes in sleep, we were all greatly fatigued." They worked continuously, but when the glow of pre-dawn crept into the sky, they realized many soldiers were still in the works. The coming of daylight would unmask everything: the entrenchments were almost empty, droves of boats were passing back and forth from Brooklyn to York Island, and waiting troops were lined up at the docks. Howe surely would attack

The withdrawal of rebel troops after the Battle of Long Island in 1776.

immediately. In the gloaming of early dawn, Tallmadge and his comrades were "very anxious for our own safety" when "a dense fog began to rise, and it seemed to settle in a peculiar manner over both encampments . . . and so very dense was the atmosphere that I could scarcely discern a man at six yards distance."

Tallmadge's regiment was grateful to be ordered to the docks for embarkation. Their relief was short-lived, however, for headquarters hurriedly sent an aide to order them into the front lines to join the rearguard. As did Hand's Pennsylvanians, the Connecticut men turned about and took their assigned positions.

The sun rose, but the fog remained sheltering and thick. Orders came at last for the Connecticut men to withdraw to the Brooklyn ferry slip. Tallmadge regretfully tied his horse to a post near the dock—it was his favorite mount—then accompanied his regiment filing toward the water's edge. When they got there, however, they found all the boats were gone. They had taken loads to New York City. Tallmadge and the others could only wait, well aware they might never get out. It seemed a long wait, surrounded by that impenetrable fog, listening to the lap of the river, not knowing what would happen next, or whether enemy forward parties were already coming into the empty American lines.

Then a boat materialized from the mist. And another. Then several more, until dozens of craft handled by the Massachusetts fishermen were making their way to the slip to get Tallmadge's regiment, among the last to leave, although there was at least one more person yet to go: Tallmadge thought he "saw General Washington on the ferry stairs when I stepped onto one of the last boats that received the troops."

It was a miraculous escape.

Every man, most of the army's artillery, and tons of supplies were transported that night. The fortunate rise of the fog played a crucial part, but the embarkation succeeded thanks to determined leadership and devoted soldiers. In fact, there was even a bit more time left, as the lingering fog gave Tallmadge pause to think about the favorite horse he had left behind. He found some willing volunteers and dared to recross, fetching the horse on board just as British gunshots sounded at the unoccupied front lines. Tallmadge "got off some distance into the river before the enemy appeared in Brooklyn."

The evacuation of the Continental Army from Long Island in August 1776 was called a scandalous disgrace for the royal forces, with General Howe resoundingly blamed for being too timid. Nevertheless, it was one of the best-executed tactical withdrawals in the history of war. Before the Revolution was over, General Washington would have more such hair's-breadth escapes.

THE ONE NOT THERE

*O*N THE AFTERNOON OF DECEMBER 4, 1783, Colonel Benjamin Tallmadge could look out a sun-filled window of Fraunces Tavern toward the East River and see where other war exploits had taken place. In those first gloomy days after the Long Island defeat, the Continental Army had regrouped to fight again, losing, and then fleeing from overpowering odds. The young dragoon with his favorite horse was invaluable to Washington as a hard-riding scout. The disastrous campaign of 1776 was not the last time Tallmadge would fight on Long Island, though it remained firmly in enemy hands throughout the war. He crossed the Sound as a spy master for Washington, and also led slashing amphibious raids against enemy strong points on the island.

Tallmadge knew that another Connecticut man in Fraunces Tavern could also gaze out from the Long Room and think about espionage: Lieutenant-colonel William Hull. Not that Hull had been a spy or ever would have considered such a repulsive role. Rather, he had been a reliable and courageous infantry commander who had served since the Boston siege until today. Hull's espionage remembrance was, instead, of a dear friend and former roommate at Yale, a charming and intelligent young man he had urgently tried to talk out of spying for Washington.

William Hull's remembrance was of Nathan Hale.

*W*ASHINGTON HAD A DESPERATE NEED for intelligence that September of 1776, as General Howe on Long Island prepared for another strike against the rebels on York Island. Both sides were sending out spies, each watchful that the other's agents were intercepted. Washington found himself without enough reconnaissance, and the answer was to hastily organize a corps of New England rangers and scouts. Nathan Hale, a twenty-one-year-old captain of the 7th Connecticut, was one of them.

Washington needed more than New England scouts, however, for good intelligence about the enemy's advances was not enough. Spies had to be found immediately, men who would go behind the British lines in civilian clothes, observe, and return with precise information about enemy dispositions and preparations. What were the opposing soldiers talking about among themselves? What were their rumors, their day-to-day routines in camps and garrisons? Where were their cannons parked, their boats collected, their generals headquartered? Who was coming and going at headquarters?

When Washington asked the officers of the New England Rangers to go behind the lines, none would volunteer for such duty, for a spy was a liar, a betrayer of confidences, a dishonorable sneak. These men had enlisted as bold, honest soldiers, risking death with a pure heart. Yet, for all that, one finally stepped forward. It was Nathan Hale, the youngest ranger officer, who said, "I will undertake it."

William Hull, Hale's brother officer and longtime friend, tried to talk him out of it, saying that such ignoble service was not required of any soldier. Hull insisted his friend's "nature was too frank and open for deceit and disguise." Further: "Who respects the character of spy?" Besides, if caught, he would be hanged like a dog.

Before the war, Tallmadge, Hull, and Hale had been close friends, three bright young men from leading Connecticut families, recent graduates of Yale College with the world at their feet. It was without question that they would join up to fight in the militia at Boston in 1775, willing to die in battle for their homes, families, and liberty. They idealized death with honor, with glory.

When the war began in 1775, Nathan Hale had resigned his attractive position as a schoolteacher in New London, and

An infantry commander in most of the key northern battles, including Trenton and Saratoga, William Hull, of Connecticut, remained with the army as second-in-command of the only American regiment still in existence at the time of Washington's farewell.

in doing had so broken the hearts of many young ladies. Some of them had been his adoring pupils at special early-morning classes he held for girls before the boys came in for the regular school session. After joining up, he served in the lines at Boston and later was stationed at Long Island. Just before the defeat, his unit had been pulled out to garrison a fort north of New York City. Disappointed not to have seen action, he felt somewhat useless, wasted, as the army was driven from Long Island to vulnerable positions on York Island.

Hale was resolved to go behind the lines, for he felt he had done nothing worthwhile as a soldier this past year under arms. Hull later said his friend believed "he owed his country the accomplishment of an object so important, and so much desired by the commander of her armies, and he knew of no other mode of obtaining the information than by assuming a disguise and passing into the enemy's camp." Hale had the highest of patriotic motives, which compelled him to do even the most distasteful duty willingly.

Failing in rational arguments, William Hull simply begged him not to go; but Hale did go, and they never saw each other again.

*H*ALE WENT BY SLOOP FROM Norwalk to Long Island and made his way into the British lines, posing as an unemployed schoolteacher—which in fact he was. Observing troop movements and defenses, he scribbled notes in Latin, secreting the papers in his shoe. On September 15, a few days after Hale arrived on Long Island, Howe attacked New York, driving Washington out of the city to new defensive positions on high ground near the village of Harlem.

Hale's mission on Long Island was useless now, so he found his way across to York Island, again moving through the military encampments. Then the city caught fire. A terrible blaze raged for four days, making hundreds homeless before it was brought under control by the combined efforts of soldiers, sailors, and civilians. A number of suspected arsonists were killed on the spot by enraged soldiers and loyalists, who dreaded more fires that could wipe out the entire city. Howe's army and loyalist supporters now were on the lookout for spies and traitors, and every stranger became suspect. What was worse, there were people on the enemy's side who knew Hale well and might recognize him.

He never got back to General Washington.

Captured on the night of September 21, the papers in his shoe discovered, Hale was immediately brought before General Howe himself. Howe was still bitter about Washington's escape from Long Island, and was furious that the rebels yet stood their ground, even winning a small victory of sorts by repelling a British advance at Harlem Heights. Washington's force had cut down Scottish and Hessian soldiers with artillery fire, and even had made a counterattack, as if they had some hope of ultimate success. Chafing Howe all the more was the smoke drifting northward to his headquarters in the Beekman mansion, as New York still smoldered from the fire. Hale admitted he was a spy, so without any trial, Howe summarily ordered him taken away to be hanged the next morning.

On the afternoon of the execution, William Hull heard about it from Captain Alexander Hamilton, commander of the gun battery that had repulsed the British at Harlem Heights. Hamilton had just met a redcoat officer who arrived in the rebel camp under a flag of truce and had told of Hale's death. Heartbroken, Hull had to know what had happened to his friend, so he was grateful to be invited to join the conference with the man, Captain John Montressor, a military engineer. Montressor was well-known to many New Yorkers, for he had been a resident of the province more than twenty years, all his children born here. He had commanded the first British troops to discover that the Americans had escaped Long Island a few weeks earlier.

Montressor came through the lines today to bring a communication from Howe to Washington for arranging an exchange of prisoners, but most of all he wanted the opportunity to report the bad news to acquaintances of Nathan

The Great Fire of 1776 in New York City, picturing soldiers beating suspected arsonists.

Hale. The redcoat officer had been with Hale before and during the execution, had spoken with him, and offered shelter in his own tent while the gallows was being readied. Montressor had brought Hale paper and pen to write his last letters—letters stolen by the brutal loyalist provost marshal in charge of the hanging.

Now Hull listened as Montressor told of Hale's courage, his "consciousness of rectitude and high intentions." Hale had made a speech as he ascended to the noose. Yes, the volatile young scholar would have made a speech. Always clear-headed in front of an audience, he had been good with words, especially when excited by the notion of fighting tyranny. Nor had Hale ever feared death. Once, in a small boat during a storm, as others cringed, he had laughed: "I am to be hanged, not drowned!"

When off duty at New York, they had liked to meet at taverns such as Fraunces's, these three friends of the Yale class of '73—Tallmadge, Hull, and Hale. Even when the British were massing around New York City in such force that only madmen or diehard young rebels would nonchalantly look forward to battle with them, these three drank and joked and sang. In those days they would have been inspired by a stirring song like the immensely popular "Ballad of Nathan Hale," which was a favorite of Americans in the years after that momentous 1776.

> *Five minutes were given, short moments, no more,*
> *For him to repent; for him to repent;*
> *He prayed for his mother, he asked not another.*
> *To Heaven he went; to heaven he went.*

* * *

The faith of a martyr, the tragedy showed,
  As he trod the last stage; as he trod the last stage.
And Britons will shudder at gallant Hale's blood,
  As his words do presage; as his words do presage.

Before departing, Montressor had recited Nathan Hale's last words for Hull: "I only regret that I have but one life to lose for my country."

DEFEAT, RETREAT, ATTACK

*M*OST OF THE MEN AT FRAUNCES TAVERN had been there when the British struck hard that autumn of 1776, driving the Americans northward, where they rallied only to be struck again, their forts falling, thousands taken prisoner. Washington barely kept the army from being wiped out as it was driven back at White Plains, suffered the disastrous loss of Fort Washington and Fort Lee, hustled exhausted in retreat through north Jersey to New Brunswick, with the guns of Knox and Hamilton holding off hot pursuit while the remnant of the dwindling force crossed rivers.

General George Clinton wrote about the "most horrid" conditions the army suffered, lying "in cold trenches," without shelter. "Daily on fatigue, making redoubts, fleches, abatis and lines, and retreating from them and the little temporary huts before they are well finished." Clinton worried that this relentless draining of their strength would "destroy our little army without fighting."

In Washington's retreat of 1776, the only good news—and it was remarkably good—came in October, when General Philip Schuyler, Horatio Gates, and Colonel Benedict Arnold stopped the powerful British advance down Lake Champlain from Canada. The enemy had been commanded by Carleton, seconded by General John Burgoyne, who eventually would have his own opportunity to lead an army down that same invasion route. Yet even the success of Schuyler and Arnold had not been enough to reverse the grave situation facing the commander-in-chief in New Jersey. Washington's distress was intensified by the outcries of the frightened Congress at Philadelphia. Its members were losing confidence in him, some of them wishing General Charles Lee, his second-in-command, were in charge.

There soon followed veiled insubordination by Lee, a boastful former British dragoon officer who was convinced that only he was fit to be the first general of the Continental Army. He had about seven thousand men under his command, protecting New England, a force Washington wanted to unite with his own. When the commander-in-chief requested him to come south, Lee made lame excuses that he dare not move, lest the enemy advance northward. Washington asked him even more urgently to come, but still Lee dallied, apparently willing to see the general irretrievably defeated, after which Lee would rush to the rescue. Lee's allies in Congress were secretly promoting him as America's savior.

The Continental Army needed good generals, but also good junior officers. Some able men were coming into positions of leadership, but not fast enough to make up for the deficiencies of many others, who often had been political appointments or were too old to be as effective as they had been in the French and Indian War. In a letter to his brother, Henry Knox lamented the shortcomings of Washington's officer corps: Knox set high standards and had a vision for a national military academy.

"The general is as worthy a man as breathes, but he cannot do everything nor be everywhere. He wants good assistants. There is a radical evil in our army—the lack of officers. We ought to have men of merit in the most extensive and unlimited sense of the word. Instead of which, the bulk of the officers of the army are a parcel of ignorant, stupid men, who might make tolerable soldiers, but are bad officers; and until Congress forms an establishment to induce men proper for the purpose to leave their usual employments and enter the service, it is ten to one they will be beat till they are heartily sick of it."

Inexperienced and incompetent American officers were troublesome enough, but the so-called experts, like Charles Lee and the former British Army supply officer General Horatio Gates, were turning out to be even more difficult, for they were intriguers. Believing they could lead the army better than Washington, they cultivated supporters in Congress—including John Adams—and corresponded with each other, regularly criticizing Washington and scheming to replace him. Washington knew there were such budding conspiracies, but he had to ignore them because there was too much to be done keeping his little force in existence.

By December 1776, after retreating across New Jersey, Washington, Knox, and all the rest were indeed heartily sick of defeat. With the enemy under General Charles Cornwallis close on his heels, Washington brought about four thousand ragged and starving men across the Delaware River above Philadelphia. The core of his army was saved, and now he directly ordered Lee to come south and join him near Philadelphia, "whose loss must prove of the most fatal consequences to the cause of America." Lee moved only reluctantly, slowly. So slowly that in mid-December he dallied at an inn with a woman in western New Jersey, and there the British captured him. Ironically, he was taken—in his dressing gown and slippers—by dragoons from his former regiment while he was writing a conspiratorial letter to Gates, in which he described Washington as "a certain man [who] is most damnably deficient."

At first, the capture of Lee appeared to be another disastrous loss for the failing American cause, but it proved to be a blessing in disguise, for Washington was rid of an influential, undermining rival. Yet, for all that he had been relieved of Lee—the reliable Alexander McDougall assuming much of Lee's responsibilities—Washington was not much stronger militarily, not even when elements of Lee's army finally joined him. Over on the east side of the Delaware, well-armed, well-fed British and Hessian forces settled down for the winter in several comfortable bases. They expected to snuff out the rebellion by spring, leisurely brushing the Continental Army aside and marching into Philadelphia, for Washington had not enough left to fight with.

Or so they thought.

*C*HRISTMAS DAY, 1776. The cause was at its lowest ebb. Only six thousand troops were at hand—two thousand of them recently arrived, green militia from Pennsylvania. Most of the men with experience would depart on January 1, when their enlistments were up. Who could blame them?

They had endured much. In twelve weeks, the army had lost five battles and five thousand men killed, wounded, or captured. Most of its artillery had been lost and virtually all the supplies, with nothing much in the way of replacement coming from Congress. The men were ragged, always cold, and half-starved in their hurriedly built encampments on the west bank of the Delaware. Knox had managed to save some field guns, thanks to his clever innovation of building lighter gun carriages so the artillery would be more maneuverable. With excellent battery commanders like Alexander Hamilton, the army's strongest arm by far was its artillery, whose guns were at the heart of Washington's plan to counterattack the enemy at Trenton.

It would begin tonight, in the midst of icy rain, and be carried out by men who had to wrap rags around their heads for hats and around their feet for shoes. Moving the main body of twenty-four hundred soldiers to a ford nine miles above Trenton, Washington ordered another, smaller, force to cross below the town. They were to unite for the assault, which would trap about a thousand Hessian troops garrisoned in the village. As with the Long Island escape in August, part of this movement was carried out in darkness and would again be in the hands of the resourceful fishermen from Massachusetts.

Using shallow-draft Durham boats, flat-bottomed and with

prows at both ends, the fishermen methodically ferried the expedition across the stream. Abruptly, the weather turned sharply colder. New ice formed at the edge of the river and around the boats, floes rapping and banging against their sides. The wind picked up, chilling the huddled bodies of soldiers clad in whatever they could scrounge. Yet the troops were sober, determined. They could not fail. Once the attack began, there was nowhere to retreat.

A congressional visitor to Washington's headquarters in this time happened to notice a piece of paper that had fallen to the floor in the general's quarters. On it Washington had written, "Victory or Death." The countersign to the army's password on the day of the attack on Trenton was "Victory or death." The men who crossed the icy river with George Washington this night were sworn to that.

In addition to its excellent artillery, the army had another factor in its favor: most of the men were battle-hardened, tested by adversity and tempered in the worst of conditions. Though shocked and driven by the best troops in the world, and whipped repeatedly, still they were not beaten, even in retreat. More than once they had withstood frontal attacks and massed volleys. They had even driven the enemy once. And here they were, still together, having fought their way through, believing in each other. Most important of all, their general believed in them, even if Congress did not and had fled from Philadelphia to Baltimore. Washington was willing to lead them on the attack, and they rose to that.

During those bitterly cold hours crossing the Delaware River, Washington inspired them. He calmly ordered the movements of men and guns and horses into the boats, quietly giving commands to Knox, who in turn called them out to the troops. The general still had a sense of humor. As he watched the portly Knox clamber into a craft, Washington declared, "Shift your tail, Knox, and trim the boat!" All the men who heard it laughed.

They felt like soldiers, and as they gathered their strength for this gamble of an assault in enemy territory, they knew Washington was a general. He did not break, not even under successive defeats. He was revered by the rank and file as never before.

*I*N THE REBEL ARMY WAS writer Thomas Paine, an Englishman who had emigrated to America in 1774 and served throughout the retreat across New Jersey. Paine had recently composed an essay, laying his paper on the head of a drum and writing by the light of a campfire. Published on December 19, it told of the army's struggle, beginning with:

> These are the times that try men's souls. The summer soldier and the sunshine patriot will, in this crisis, shrink from the service of their country; but he that stands it now deserves the love and thanks of man and woman. Tyranny, like hell, is not easily conquered; yet we have this consolation with us, that the harder the conflict, the more glorious the triumph.

Paine noted the general's fortitude, and his "mind that can even flourish upon care." Washington already had told Congress that he would fight on, if he must, in the wilds of

The Hessian commander, Von Rall, is dying of his wounds as he surrenders to Washington after the Battle of Trenton in December 1776.

western Pennsylvania, or farther off in the Ohio country. He would not surrender while he yet breathed. At the same time, he wrote home to his estate manager at Mount Vernon, telling him to discreetly make contingency plans to flee into the northwest wilderness.

In a recent council, New Hampshire's John Stark, a senior captain of the renowned Rogers Rangers in the last war, had bluntly told the general, "Your men have too long been accustomed to place their dependence for safety upon spades and pickaxes." Indeed, even the enemy mocked the rebel penchant for building fortifications, singing a song entitled "The Burrowing Yankees," and asserting that rebels could never fight in the open field face-to-face with the British or their Hessian auxiliaries.

Colonel Stark added, "If ever you expect to establish the independence of these states, you must teach them to place dependence upon their firearms and courage."

Now back on the New Jersey side after their harrowing crossing, the troops formed their columns and advanced at the first light of dawn. As on Long Island, mist and rain helped screen their movements, but it was very cold. When reports came in that the black powder for muskets was too wet to fire, the general replied, "Use the bayonet. I am resolved to take Trenton."

Bayonets and cannon.

The advance toward Trenton and the sleeping Hessians was determined and decisive. Though word arrived that the other rebel force had given up trying to cross the icy river, Washington pressed on. It was a "terrible night for the soldiers," said one officer, but added that he heard no one complain. Advance elements quickly overpowered enemy sentry posts and pickets before they could give the alarm. On the men plodded, heads down against the harsh wind. One man looked up to see Washington ride slowly alongside the column, saying in a "deep and solemn" voice, "Soldiers, keep by your officers. For God's sake, keep by your officers!"

Suddenly, the general's horse lost its footing on a slippery bank; the soldier was startled to see its hind legs begin to go out, until Washington forcibly "seized his horse's mane, and the horse recovered."

The troops pressed on into a hailstorm that stung their faces. When they formed up to attack the town, the storm was put at their backs, so it would be hailing in the faces of the enemy. Surprise was on the American side. The eighteen field guns, drawn by horses, moved with a rapidity that was unheard of in the conventional army of the day. With precise movements, Hamilton placed his artillery wheel to wheel, aiming down the streets of the village.

The alarm went up. Startled enemy guards opened fire.

The Hessians were shocked that the cowardly Americans, "those country clowns," were daring to attack them. Whether or not they had been drinking and merry-making the day before, the Hessians were tough professionals, who rushed into the streets ready to fight—only to be staggered by a devastating artillery barrage. Many fell, but the rest struggled to recover and did not panic, even though more were shot down as they hurried from the houses. Again and again rebel cannon fired, and the streets ran red with Hessian blood, but the enemy kept their discipline and rallied.

Hessian gunners tried to reach their cannon, but the Americans blasted most of them down. Those who made it to their stations exchanged salvos with the rebel guns, but soon found themselves attacked by infantry. One force of attackers, led by Virginia infantry lieutenant James Monroe, defied the enemy grapeshot and captured an artillery crew. The main body of Hessians, surrounded, attempted to form up in the teeth of withering artillery fire, but the Americans never gave them a chance. American infantry attacked relentlessly from every side and—as Washington predicted and Stark recommended—the fighting was with the bayonet, hand-to-hand, man-to-man, face-to-face. The enemy had never imagined this possible.

Still, the Hessians did not give up, and some counterattacked, trying to fight their way out, only to find the rebel artillery had quickly shifted positions and again was blasting at them. Even the most courageous could not endure it. They were driven into huddled groups, bewildered by this unexpected American aggressiveness. Then their commander was shot from the saddle, mortally wounded. It was all over in less than an hour. The enemy surrendered, more than eight hundred of them, with six officers and about thirty soldiers dead, many wounded. Washington's most audacious gamble thus far had succeeded, with only two Americans lost—both having frozen to death—and four wounded, including James Monroe and Samuel Webb, though neither seriously. This was Webb's third wound of the war. Washington himself narrowly avoided a wound, as his sword hilt was struck by a bullet that passed between two of his fingers.

At Trenton, the plan of attack had been well-conceived, the execution by the troops just as good. Even though the supporting force downriver never got across to join the assault, Washington had gone in anyway, because retreat was no longer an option.

However inspiring was the Trenton victory, perhaps the most telling result was the enhanced reputation of the officers. The victory was largely because of their skill, courage, and adept handling of men, guns, and boats. Now Henry Knox could reconsider his previous harsh assessment of the officer corps, an assessment made just four months earlier. Washington might have only a small army, poorly armed and scarcely supplied, but he had found the right men to lead it.

Some were generals and colonels, others junior officers. The best included Knox, Nathanael Greene, William Alexander (Lord Stirling), Alexander Hamilton, Hugh Mercer, John Stark, Samuel Shaw, Philip van Cortlandt, Alexander Scammell, Edward Hand, Samuel Webb, William Hull, William Maxwell, Horatio Gates, James Monroe, John Haslet. Other good ones were either in the North, defending New England and the invasion route through New York from Canada, or in the South, fighting loyalists and defending the coastal cities from expected attack: Philip Schuyler, George and James Clinton, Alexander McDougall, Benedict Arnold, Arthur St. Clair, James Sullivan, John Paterson, Benjamin Lincoln, Henry Jackson, David Humphreys, Anthony Wayne, Jedediah Huntington, Nicholas Fish, Richard Varick, Benjamin Tallmadge, Benjamin Walker, Francis Marion, Daniel Morgan, John Lamb...

Many more able officers were coming into their own. Those with Washington had tasted victory at Trenton and wanted another. The redcoat force quartered near Princeton was just a day's march away, but Washington knew better than to overreach. As his exhilarated army collected its booty of weapons, ammunition, and Hessian supplies and goods, the general ordered captured casks of rum to be burst open in the streets to prevent drunkenness, which would have destroyed discipline and might have exposed the men to a surprise counterattack. After the Americans crossed back over the wintry Delaware with their prisoners and spoils, they returned to the welcome warmth of campfires and savored what they had done.

Someone wrote a song about how the troops felt just then:

> *We'll drink our own liquor, our brandy from peaches,*
> *A fig for the English, they may all kiss our breeches,*
> *Those blood-sucking, beer-drinking puppies retreat;*
> *But our peach-brandy fellows can never be beat.*

AN ELUSIVE OLD FOX

*I*N THE YEARS BEFORE THE WAR BEGAN at Lexington and Concord in 1775, Samuel Shaw was a proper young man of wealthy family living in a Boston home where two British officers were quartered. As the relations between civilians and redcoats steadily worsened, Samuel had to suffer sitting at the same table with Major John Pitcairn, the Scottish-born commander of the marine detachment—who admittedly was likable, for a redcoat officer—and one Lieutenant Wragg, who despised Americans and flatly said so.

By 1783, those days likely seemed long ago to the war-weary Major Shaw as he waited for Washington to appear in the Long Room. It had been only moments since he and the others had arrived, but everyone was uneasy to think of seeing His Excellency for the last time. Shaw was in company with Major-general Knox, to whom he had been a valued aide-de-camp since June of 1782, and in whose artillery command he had served since January 1776. Shaw would have joined up even earlier, but he had been under age, and his father had refused him permission to go.

As the events of the 1770s had built toward fighting, so had the relationship between young Samuel and Lieutenant Wragg. Then came the day when, at a family meal without Major Pitcairn present, the lieutenant had called Americans cowards. Samuel had angrily challenged Wragg to a duel, and had been accepted. Things went so far that formal arrangements for the affair of honor were well along in preparation before Pitcairn heard about it. He interfered and persuaded his hot-headed lieutenant, either by force of reason or by direct command, to apologize to the family for his rudeness. Apology accepted, there had been no duel, but Shaw was eager to go to war against the redcoats.

Then, in the spring of 1775, came the final break: Lexington and Concord. The intrepid Pitcairn was one of the embattled British commanders who barely prevented utter rout as the rebel militiamen drove the redcoats back into the city. Excited now, Samuel had begged his father's permission to leave the city and join the militia forces, but still he was forbidden. That October, Samuel turned twenty-one and became of age. Now, with his father's approval and influence, he applied to General Washington for a position as lieutenant in the artillery.

So began the distinguished career of Major Samuel Shaw, who remained in Washington's army until Evacuation Day.

A Boston native from a leading Massachusetts family, Samuel Shaw was a fine artillery officer who served throughout the war; in 1782 he became aide-de-camp to Knox and was a close observer of events in the Newburgh conspiracy.

Recently he had been given letters from both His Excellency and Knox commending his meritorious service. Of all the engagements, from Boston to Yorktown, few were more memorable to Samuel Shaw than the Battle of Princeton, when Washington outwitted the formidable Lord Cornwallis and the entire British Army in the Jerseys.

Shaw had distinguished himself at the guns during the Trenton victory, and was promoted from first lieutenant to captain in time for Princeton.

*W*ASHINGTON GAVE HIS MEN only a few days to rest after Trenton, for many were scheduled to depart homeward, their enlistments up on the first of the year, 1777. Some militia and new recruits were coming in, thanks to the heartening victory at Trenton, but the general needed the experienced men to stand by him in another invasion into New Jersey.

One by one, he paraded the "old" regiments, and rode before their ranks, addressing them personally, thanking them, but saying they could do even more for their country at this moment than at any other, if only they would remain with him.

With, as spectators, Massachusetts officers such as Knox and newly promoted artillery captain Samuel Shaw, Washington paraded the New Englanders, who were about to leave. Naturally, the troops were flooded with thoughts of home and loved ones, of good food, blessed peace and quiet and safety, and of well-deserved laurels after their victory. These thoughts mixed with Washington's moving words and the force of his personality as he spoke. Knox and Shaw had often seen the general do exactly this with time-expired regiments at Boston in 1775, but with only limited success, as most men had gone home anyway.

Now, he asked them to stay longer, and the drums beat for volunteers to step forward.

No one did.

Washington wheeled his horse, shouting, "My brave fellows, you have done all I asked you to do and more than could be reasonably expected..." He appealed once more for them to stay with him, and the drums beat again for volunteers.

No one moved, but men glanced uneasily at one another.

The general cried out, "The present is emphatically the crisis which is to decide our destiny!"

The drums rolled.

One man, then another, turned to comrades in the ranks, saying he would stay if they would.

They did. To Washington's delight, most of the New England men, most of the army, extended their enlistments another six weeks, just enough time to take a good crack at Lord Cornwallis, who was back in New Jersey with reinforcements after canceling his voyage home to England to see his sick wife.

$\mathcal{B}$EFORE THEY HEARD OF THE VICTORY at Trenton, the beleaguered Congress tried to cope with the deepening emergency by taking the desperate step of authorizing Washington "full, ample, and complete powers" to raise sixteen new battalions of infantry and also new units of horse, artillery, and engineers. Of key importance was the authority to appoint his own officers, rather than having states control that vital prerogative. This meant he was truly a continental commander-in-chief, with the power a general needed to prosecute a war properly—power that republicans understandably dreaded to see vested in any military man.

"Happy it is for this country," Congress wrote him, "that the general of their forces can be safely intrusted with the most unlimited power, and neither personal security, liberty, nor property be in the least degree endangered thereby."

Washington would take the first opportunity to reorganize the army. Yet Congress controlled the finances, which meant they had the power either to fund his various efforts or not, as it suited the continental union or, just as often, each state's particular objectives.

In the meantime, there was Cornwallis, and the rebel army had just six weeks of extended enlistment in which to move against him. Afterward, Washington would decide where his army would spend the winter. Pennsylvania was too remote from occupied New York City; the general believed the war would not end until New York was retaken, and he wanted to remain within striking distance. Since New Jersey was full of enemy soldiers, he would have to fight his way through to the best winter cantonment.

$\mathcal{B}$Y JANUARY 1, 1777, WASHINGTON had recrossed the Delaware, as if inviting an attack from the army of six or seven thousand under Lord Cornwallis, who alertly seized the chance. Washington withdrew slowly from the advancing enemy and dug in behind a stream. Cornwallis moved to attack. At Washington's orders, American units slowed the enemy's progress by skirmishing on his flanks so that he could not get close enough to make an assault before dark.

That was what Washington wanted. The enemy was meant to believe the rebels were foolishly allowing themselves to be hemmed in with their backs against the Delaware River. The British camped for the night across the creek, Cornwallis saying he had Washington, "the old fox," right where he wanted him: "We'll go over and bag him in the morning."

That night, with Shaw and the other artillery officers making sure the wheels of their guns, carts, and wagons were muffled, Washington slipped his army away, leaving campfires burning brightly to fool His Lordship. Again the weather worked in Washington's favor, as roads that had been muddy all day suddenly froze hard, affording passage for the artillery. Weary, sleepy men trudged through the night, some falling asleep against their comrades whenever the column paused, which was often, to let wheeled vehicles through.

Washington kept them moving. He was after another swift success, and meant to surprise Cornwallis's rear guard of three regiments protecting the supply depot in Princeton. If all went well, the army would drive on to New Brunswick, capture or destroy the vast enemy stores stockpiled there, and perhaps even make off with the seventy thousand pounds sterling held in Cornwallis's war chest. With that kind of hard money in hand, Washington believed he could "put an end to the war."

The American advance troops under General Hugh Mercer ran into the British just southwest of Princeton. The action quickly became hot, with Mercer's men outnumbered by aggressive enemy regulars eager for a fight and intending to defeat the rebels decisively. The British were convinced that the Hessian loss at Trenton was a result of their commander's incompetence, not American prowess. As the battle raged, artillery batteries fired at each other from close range. Guns were won and lost in charge and counter-charge, with men from one state willingly fighting under officers from another. The courage of several hundred troops and a battery of artillery from the best families of Philadelphia was prominent throughout. Commanded by Captain David Neal, the Philadelphia guns came under irresistible assault.

General Mercer ordered a retreat, then his horse was shot and fell. Mercer fought on foot with his sword, but died under enemy bayonets. The moment was crucial, the patriots retreating, but Neal gallantly fired two devastating rounds of grapeshot with telling effect before the enemy overran his guns and killed him. Up came Washington with the Continental infantry and artillery. As the infantry deployed into line of battle, Knox's artillery fired salvo after salvo of grapeshot, slowing the redcoat advance, then forcing them to retreat. At this crucial moment, Washington was revealed as utterly fearless in action, and some of his men might have wondered whether he was divinely protected. He galloped on his white horse across the face of the front ranks, turned at the center and called on the troops to advance. When both armies were within thirty yards, Washington shouted for his men to fire, though he was between the armies. They did. The general was an open target, coolly astride his big horse, bullets flying everywhere, with only the drifting gunsmoke offering concealment from the enemy. In the heat of battle, one of his aides could not bear to watch, expecting to see his beloved general fall.

A young soldier wrote home to his wife about that awful, glorious moment: "I shall never forget what I felt at Princeton on his account, when I saw him brave all the dangers of the field and his important life hanging as it were by a single hair with a thousand deaths flying around him."

More than a hundred redcoats took cover in Nassau Hall at the College of New Jersey, and Hamilton's battery sent in a few rounds to drive them out. A cannonball is said to have smashed a portrait of King George II before a white flag appeared at a window.

The fight at Princeton was brief but bloody, the British learning what the Hessians at Trenton had discovered about American aggressiveness. In less than an hour, the engagement was done, and almost three hundred enemy troops were

Immediately after his triumph at Trenton, Washington outmaneuvered Cornwallis and defeated his rear guard near Princeton.

killed, wounded or prisoner. The routed survivors fled toward Trenton and New Brunswick, leaving the Americans in command of the field, suffering only forty-four casualties, although these included the worthy General Mercer and Colonel Haslet, who both died. The road lay virtually open to New Brunswick, seventeen miles away, but the army was completely spent, and there were no fresh reinforcements to be had. By now, the outfoxed Cornwallis, with more than five thousand men, was coming in pursuit.

The rebel fox headed northward into the New Jersey hills, where he fortified at Morristown and went into winter camp. He was just twenty-five miles from New York, close enough to strike if the chance came his way, far enough to avoid surprise by Howe's main army, and perched commandingly above the road to Philadelphia. The campaign finished, the ragged Continentals had risen from the ashes of defeat to fight again, and to win twice. The success of the northern army against Carleton and Washington's two quick victories altered the balance more in favor of the Americans. The rebels had time on their side, if only Congress did not push Washington into making rash decisions for the sake of victories in the field.

*T*HE ARMY AT MORRISTOWN BEGAN TO MELT away as men went home, enlistments up, and Washington would have to maintain the illusion of strength and readiness all through that hungry winter. Howe and Cornwallis must never know his force was diminished to only a thousand Continentals and a couple of thousand willing but inept militia volunteers.

When springtime came, the campaigns would renew. In

the north, General Burgoyne replaced Carleton as field commander of the British army based in Canada, and he would again invade New York State, striking toward the Hudson Valley to divide New England from the rest of the country. In the South, loyalist forces were strong and active, always a threat to open the way for British military occupation. In the mid-Atlantic states, Washington would be contending with Howe's overwhelming force, and, as if this burden were not enough, he would also have to wrestle with Congress for his men's food and pay.

Congress was weak and divided, and because it could not tax the states it had little hard money available to finance the army. Moreover, the members dreaded an army that was too strong, and Congress constantly tried to keep Washington's influence and power in check, whether by refusing to lengthen enlistment periods or by appointing quartermasters who were politically malleable and so kept a tight grip on military supplies and pay. Some members of Congress undermined Washington by lavishing attention on other generals, such as Horatio Gates and captive Charles Lee, praising them at Washington's expense, and trying to build them up in the eyes of the country.

Thanks to his triumphs at Trenton and Princeton, Washington would have new recruits by springtime, but the enemy would be more dangerous than ever, for they had learned a military lesson about underestimating their foes. For one thing, the American artillery under Knox, with battery commanders such as captains Hamilton and Shaw, had astonished the British by its unexpected skill and maneuverability. In a day when the bayonet charge was famed and feared as the most decisive weapon of war, Knox's innovative and devastating use of artillery had been crucial for both victories. At this time, the British dragoon colonel who had captured General Lee wrote home to his father about the rebels, saying, "though it was once the fashion of this army to treat them in the most contemptible light, they are now become a formidable enemy."

THE PEN OF THE ARMY

𝓕EW MEN IN THE FRAUNCES TAVERN Long Room had been more essential to His Excellency than Alexander Hamilton. None had so close a relationship with Washington.

Now that the British were finally leaving New York, Hamilton was setting out on a course of nation-building, with the odds for success as daunting as those faced by the Revolutionary army eight years earlier. As they had during the armed conflict, the New Yorkers in this room would continue to influence the future of their state and the shaky American confederation. Their farewell to His Excellency would perhaps be the last time they would be united in spirit.

Party interests had opened a rift between Hamilton and Governor Clinton, and long-standing political tensions were as strong as ever now that peace was assured and people were ready to rebuild. Just a few days ago, Hamilton had opened a law office around the corner on Wall Street. Born in the British West Indies, he had come to America in late 1772, soon making a name for himself as a progressive thinker on current affairs. No sooner had he opened his office than Hamilton benefited from the patronage of returning New York Sons of Liberty. He also had the backing of Philip Schuyler, the Albany Dutch patroon, whose beautiful daughter, Betsy, Hamilton had married. Schuyler was George Clinton's strongest competitor for leadership in New York, and in 1777 had lost to him in the state's first election for governor. Schuyler backed Hamilton's vision of a federation of American states, but Clinton—called "The Father of His State"—favored an independent New York.

As Clinton and his brother, James, mingled with their former comrades-in-arms, all waiting for Washington, it was apparent that the Schuyler-Hamilton faction and the firmly established Clintons were fated to be bitter political enemies. It little mattered that throughout the war they had been effective allies and unswervingly loyal to Washington. Schuyler, who was back home in Saratoga, had masterminded the defense of the upper reaches of Hudson's River, while George Clinton, who came from Ulster County, had been the key commander responsible for holding the mid-Hudson Valley.

In his quest for power, Hamilton could count on many of the allies he had made before the war, including such men in this room as Lamb, McDougall, Richard Varick, and Nicholas Fish. Lieutenant-colonel Varick, thirty years old, had been Benedict Arnold's aide-de-camp in 1780, when the traitor had attempted to betray West Point. Surviving slander that had cast suspicion on him, too, Varick had gone on to become Washington's confidential secretary. Lieutenant-colonel Fish, just twenty-five and only half a year older than Hamilton, had been a commander of elite light infantry, and in the final assault at Yorktown had been Hamilton's second-in-command. Fish, despite his youth, was a man of rigid principles. Late in 1776, when his loyalist father and sister had arranged a meeting with him to beg that he come into occupied New York on a British pass to see his desperately ill mother, he had sadly chosen duty above family and refused to leave his post.

Schuyler, Lamb, McDougall, Varick, Fish—with such powerful New York allies as these, and with the good wishes of His Excellency himself, Hamilton intended to lead in the establishment of a national government. He well knew the adversity he faced, for four years on Washington's staff had often placed him directly in the line of political fire, revealing the power of the general's enemies in Congress and in the army as they unsuccessfully conspired and manipulated to bring the great man down.

Hamilton also had seen how Washington had outdone his opponents by sheer strength of will, by a few effective manipulations of his own, and in the end by a sublime willingness to resign as commander-in-chief if Congress did not fully support him. Congress had dared not press that issue, no matter how insecure they had been about Washington's generalship. They had known how he was loved by his troops and Congress despised.

For the American fighting man, there had been one heartening certainty throughout the conflict, and that was Washington's presence, whatever reverses occurred on the battlefield, no matter who was intriguing against him. Only once did it appear the general might leave them, and that chilling moment came at Morristown in the spring of 1777, when Alexander Hamilton first joined the headquarters staff. Washington was so sick that it was thought he might die.

*K*EY COMMANDERS, HAMILTON, AND OTHER staff officers had gathered solemnly around Washington's bed in a dimly lit room of the general's quarters. He had been feverish for several days, unable to get out of bed. Now the fever had risen, his illness taking a turn for the worse. His breathing labored and shallow, eyes glazed, and with a tight, dry cough that would not relent, Washington was unable to speak and lapsed into semi-consciousness.

All that could be done for him had been done. It was unusual for the general to be ill at all, and therefore all the more distressing to see him like this. Despite campaigning in bad weather, going without rest, and being constantly troubled by worries that long ago would have overwhelmed most men, he had never succumbed to sickness or infirmity. Indeed, it seemed that he suffered now from the awful burden of command: his soldiers were poorly fed, clothed in rags, and of late the dreaded smallpox had appeared among the army. He faced enlistments expiring and valuable men leaving, the perennial lack of support for the army from the Congress—and now the British were threatening moves into New Jersey, trying to draw him into pitched battle.

Washington seemed so ill that one of the generals standing beside the bed dared gently ask him who was to succeed him should he be unable to continue in command. The general heard. After a moment, from the depths of the fever, he compelled his eyes to go from man to man until they fell on, and fixed, Nathanael Greene, who caught his breath. Moved, Greene gripped Washington's hand, and at the same time tried to make a light remark to ease the weight of the moment.

No one, they all knew, could replace Washington.

The next day, to everyone's relief, the general was visibly better. Other good news came, for Martha Washington was on her way from Virginia to join her husband, as she had a year earlier in the winter quarters outside Boston. Seemingly by force of will, Washington recovered enough strength so that when his wife arrived on March 15 he could greet her standing on his feet, and not from a sickbed. Martha's arrival was a relief to the general's "military family," as the headquarters staff was termed. Everyone was glad she would be taking care of him.

And she did. The first thing Martha's hand turned to was a concoction of molasses and onions, which served to rid her husband of his cough.

The mood lightened, and spirits rose at headquarters as Washington recovered. The smallpox left the camp, and so the ladies of the officers were invited to come and stay a while. With the arrival of warm weather, the campaign was sure to begin, and their men would again face death or capture in the field. The impulse was to make the most of the lovely North Jersey springtime while they could. Alexander Hamilton, with his educated wit and boyish charm, was one of the most sociable of all.

*T*HE YOUTHFUL WEST INDIAN commander of the New York artillery company had been well known in those first heady days of independence in New York City. Hamilton's close-order drilling of the men had won Nathanael Greene's praise and an invitation to dinner. Meticulous with record-keeping,

Born in the British West Indies, Alexander Hamilton came to New York just before the Revolution and became friends with like-minded revolutionary firebrands Alexander McDougall, John Lamb, and Nicholas Fish.

this young "collegiate," as his sort were known, was as remarkable for his organization as for his ability with guns and courage in the field. It was General Greene who first had recommended Hamilton as an aide to Washington.

In the New York and New Jersey campaigns of 1776-77, Hamilton's outstanding direction of men and cannon had brought him to the attention of senior officers impressed with such military talent in one barely twenty years of age. Through those first years of the Revolution, Hamilton had commanded his company of artillery in battle after battle, winning the admiration of the general staff and earning the undying loyalty of his men. On one occasion in the long fighting retreat of 1776, Hamilton was observed marching alongside his cannons, seeming no more than a slender boy, hat

pulled down over his eyes, lost in thought as he absently pat-
ted his guns.

In this same time, Hamilton had turned down nomination
to the staff of General Stirling, who eventually acquired James
Monroe. Instead, Hamilton had led his men all the way to
Morristown. Washington well knew Hamilton's skill with
artillery, but what the general needed most on his staff was an
able writer, a man willing to be "confined from morning to
eve, hearing and answering the applications and letters," as he
said. The army's paperwork was overwhelming, and it too
often kept Washington busy at the expense of other essential
duties, such as inspections, developing the defensive works at
Morristown, and organizing his network of intelligence
agents from Philadelphia to New York.

The general said a writing aide had to be someone who
"can think for me, as well as execute orders." The aide usually drafted letters and speeches, and after the general's
approval, they were copied and became official. Other aides
had come and gone. At least one, a Pennsylvanian, had
resigned because he was discovered conspiring with General
Charles Lee to displace Washington; another was the well-
educated Aaron Burr of New Jersey, who had not lasted long.
Washington considered Burr "an intriguer."

When the army was not on campaign, the working hours
at the Morristown headquarters were usually from early
morning to mid-afternoon. Washington was extremely
demanding of his aides, having so much pressing correspondence—military, political, and personal—to send and answer.
Now he had found the ideal secretary in Hamilton, who soon
acquired the sense of what his general wanted to say and how
to say it. Hardworking and decisive, Hamilton took to his

duties with enthusiasm and intelligence. Eventually, he sometimes had to make independent decisions about army affairs that his commander-in-chief only afterward confirmed. Washington considered Hamilton a godsend, for no other aide was as accomplished with ink and paper. He earned the nickname "The Pen of the Army."

*A*FTER DINNER, OR IN LEISURE hours, the atmosphere at headquarters was pleasant and cheerful. No one more enjoyed good conversation, food, and drink than Washington himself, and he was always pleased to be in the company of bright, high-spirited women. The wives and grown daughters of the officers, as well as those of the many civilians and officials who visited headquarters, stimulated conviviality and fun as they arranged picnics and riding parties, teas and dances.

Washington was usually the centerpiece of these social diversions, and nearly every woman there was said to be infatuated with him. He especially enjoyed dancing, which he could keep up for three hours, nonstop, though he walked the movements rather than danced them, as most others did. He gallantly took turns with all the ladies, but appeared the most content with Martha at his side. When she talked of him to friends, Martha called him "my old man."

As efficient as young Hamilton was at headquarters in Morristown, he was also a welcome addition to the general's military family, a congenial participant in the social life of the officers and their ladies. Full of good conversation and ready humor, he "presided at the general's table," said an observer, and entertained the young women "with ease, propriety, and vivacity." Hamilton often joined the general's riding parties over gentle hills and along farm lanes around Morristown, where he observed how Washington charmed the married ladies.

One worldly Virginia lady wrote home about how delightful it was whenever the general "throws off the hero and takes on the chatty agreeable companion"—a teasingly "impudent" companion at times, she added.

A particularly attractive visitor to Morristown was Elizabeth Schuyler, accompanying her father on a mission to Congress in Philadelphia. Schuyler intended to lay out his strategy for defending the Lake Champlain-Hudson Valley corridor against Burgoyne's imminent advance from Canada. Hamilton and Betsy Schuyler were taken with each other, and Schuyler himself was impressed with the young man's abilities as an aide-de-camp—especially his knack for handling the egotistical French volunteers who were coming by the dozens to America, most of them expecting immediately to be given places as ranking officers. Hamilton spoke French fluently, and he was both polite and firm with these self-described military experts who were so sure they could outshine any American officer.

One French newcomer was the Marquis de Lafayette, who, in his late teens, was even younger than Hamilton. Unlike most of his countrymen offering their swords to Congress, however, Lafayette was modest and asked to serve Washington simply as a volunteer, without any command. He wanted only to be at the renowned general's side, even as an aide-de-camp. Hamilton and the Marquis soon became friends, and to their group was added the likable John

Laurens, a high-spirited, handsome young South Carolinian, whose father, Henry, was president of Congress and an admirer of Washington.

With the approach of the 1777 campaign season, working hours at headquarters grew much longer, and when the British began to move from New York City into New Jersey, Washington's councils of war lasted late into the night. It was time for the ladies to depart and for the army to prepare to march.

BRANDYWINE, GERMANTOWN, AND BURGOYNE

*T*HE SUMMER MONTHS OF 1777 were a one-sided chess game, as Washington cautiously responded to Howe's movements with the main British army in New Jersey and southern New York. Howe had twenty-seven thousand troops and a powerful fleet available to him, compared to eight or ten thousand Continentals in the American army, which was deployed from the Hudson highlands south to Philadelphia. Washington could call on thousands of militia to muster if a battle developed, but he wanted no battle except on terms of his choosing.

Maneuvering within striking distance of the American stronghold at Morristown, Howe tried to force a decisive battle on ground that would favor the discipline and maneuvering ability of his army. Sending strong detachments against outlying American positions in central and northern New

Jersey, he tried to tempt Washington down from the hills. Washington declined to be drawn in, and instead placed his main force so that the British would have to attack frontally. Howe would not risk that.

Meantime, with every move Howe made in New Jersey, he found angry local militia rising to swarm and sting his flanks, costing him men and making it difficult to get forage for his horses and oxen. Though the core of the rebel army did not take Howe's bait, he knew that if he dared send his army on a long and vulnerable line of march toward Philadelphia, he would be attacked in force by Washington. The British commander pretended to do just that, making an apparent move southward, then abruptly turning to meet the anticipated American pursuit. That pursuit did not come. Washington just watched from his perch, and Howe marched back, disgruntled, to Staten Island, where his army could be supplied out of reach of the harrying rebel militias.

Still, whenever the king's troops sent armed parties into New Jersey or southern New York State for food, animal fodder, or firewood, they were sure to be attacked by militia and Continentals. Both sides lost in these frequent skirmishes, but they served Washington in two major ways: the British were frustrated in supplying their forces, and the Americans learned to fight regulars. At one point Hamilton estimated the royal army had lost seven hundred men to only a hundred American casualties. Thus did the army with Washington grow steadily more sure of itself, though it was not yet a match for Howe, except on the defensive.

Part of Washington's strength was the local population's intensifying hatred of the king's troops. The British Army and its mercenaries were earning a reputation as cruel brutes who plundered civilians mercilessly, whether loyalist Tories or rebellious Whigs, as the two main American political parties were called. Washington, in contrast, treated civilians in his power wisely. Those who had taken loyalist oaths were permitted to recant and take oaths to the United States, even though as yet there was no formal American confederation. Washington also kept his men as disciplined and honorable as possible, in contrast to the king's forces, who regularly insulted, pillaged, raped, and even murdered.

While some British officers wrote home jokingly about lusty troops gang-raping American girls, Washington issued a proclamation forbidding "all the officers and soldiers of the Continental army, of the militia and all recruiting parties, [from] plundering any person whatsoever, whether Tories or others… and it is expected that humanity and tenderness to women and children will distinguish brave Americans, contending for liberty, from infamous mercenary ravagers, whether British or Hessian."

A congressional report summed up the situation, saying, "The track of the British is marked by desolation."

*W*ASHINGTON'S RESILIENCE INFURIATED and frustrated Howe, whose unproductive army was draining the British exchequer dry and causing no end to political turmoil at home. That was not enough for Congress, however, which wanted action, triumph on the battlefield.

There were plenty of political reasons to push Washington into battle, not the least of which was the value of Congress-issued currency, which rose and fell according to the success or failure of the American armies. Another rationale for precipitating action was the hope that success would persuade France to recognize America as independent, or even to lend direct military support to the rebellion. One influential New Englander wrote impatiently to John Adams at Philadelphia, complaining that he hungered "to hear of enterprises, of battles fought and victories gained on our side."

When, late in July, Howe suddenly embarked most of his army from New York City, putting it out to sea, there was anxious uncertainty at American headquarters. What would be the enemy's next move? A water-borne invasion against Philadelphia, or an assault on one of the southern coastal cities? More logically, would the fleet suddenly reappear in Hudson's River, carrying the expedition northward to unite with General Burgoyne's advance from Canada? News from the north was troubling, as Burgoyne drove toward Albany, capturing hastily abandoned Fort Ticonderoga and advancing toward Hudson's River.

New Englanders such as John Adams were furious when Ticonderoga was given up without a fight. To placate them, Congress replaced Schuyler with General Horatio Gates as northern commander. In fact, Ticonderoga had been undefendable by the small garrison that faced Burgoyne's powerful army. Wisely, Schuyler had saved his outnumbered troops to fight again. As a Yorker and a wealthy patroon, he was mistrusted by Yankees, who liked Gates because he professed to agree with pet New England political objectives, chief among which was preventing New York from claiming the Hampshire Grants after the war.

Showing remarkable courage and patriotism, the patroon remained Washington's most trusted man on the scene.

Schuyler was instrumental in seeing to it that Gates's army gathering at Saratoga was well supplied and that the region's militias mustered to join him. Washington sent some of his own precious troops north as reinforcement, and with them went valuable officers such as Philip van Cortlandt, William Hull, and Nicholas Fish. To the northern scene, too, went General Benedict Arnold as a dynamic subordinate to the overly cautious Gates. Arnold was a man the northern troops would follow into hell if he asked them. He had led many of them before: in the failed invasion of Canada at the start of the war; then in stopping the British invasion fleet on Lake Champlain last year; and in repelling a powerful raid on Connecticut earlier this spring.

While the crisis loomed in northern New York, Washington and Hamilton agreed that Burgoyne's situation was tenuous at best, and potentially catastrophic if the rebels could muster enough strength to surround him. By the time Burgoyne left garrisons and outposts to protect his lengthening supply line, he had little more than six thousand men remaining. To meet him, the Americans had five thousand Continental troops above Albany, and thousands of New York and New England militia were hurrying to join them. Schuyler provided a master delaying stroke by sending hundreds of axmen into the woods to down trees across forest trails, destroy bridges, and flood routes the British would have to follow to reach the open country of upper Hudson's River.

As far as the Americans were concerned, the most dangerous of Howe's choices that summer of 1777 would have been to go northward and join Burgoyne, laying New England open for an invasion. It was the lesser of evils when news came late in August that Howe's enormous fleet had been seen ascending the Chesapeake Bay, aiming to land south of Philadelphia, its obvious target.

At the same time, thrilling reports came in saying Burgoyne had lost hundreds of men in a defeat near Bennington, northeast of Albany. Burgoyne was in trouble, but that would not help Washington, who had to defend Philadelphia, the American seat of government. It was more important, however, to avoid having his army destroyed. The heart and soul of the American rebellion was the army. Howe could take and hold cities, but he must wipe out the rebel army to defeat the rebellion.

*T*HIS HE ATTEMPTED TO DO early in September, approaching Washington's forces, which were deployed across the Brandywine and blocking the road to Philadelphia, where Congress nervously awaited the outcome. Never before were Washington's men more confident, more ready for battle. After Trenton, Princeton, and Bennington, the Americans believed they could take on enemy regulars and win.

In the hours before the anticipated British attack, Washington rode out on reconnaissance, at one point with only one rider, a French hussar officer who had volunteered for the American service. The day was sunny, the country open and wooded. Washington was on the American-held side of the Brandywine, with woods between him and the river and screening the opposite bank, where Hessian troops under Knyphausen were positioned. With his single escort riding well ahead to scout for any surprises, Washington appraised the lay of the land so that when the fighting began he would be familiar with the terrain. After he saw what he wanted to, he rode back toward headquarters.

As the general cantered over an open field he had crossed earlier, a figure stepped out of the trees about a hundred yards off and beckoned for him to approach. Startled, Washington slowed his mount and looked at the man, but kept moving on the same line over the field. He was an easy target for a rifle-man, but the man, whoever he was, did not fire. Washington could have been more cautious because British rangers were sure to be scouting there.

Within hours, the battle was joined.

Howe feinted an attack across the Brandywine against Washington's center, while the main force of British, German, and loyalist troops marched hard and far through the summer heat to get around the American right. They fell upon it with overwhelming force, driving it back. Though most American regiments fought a reluctant withdrawal, those men who broke and ran found themselves blocked by the shouting, sword-swinging Washington, Hamilton, Lafayette, and other staff officers joined by Benjamin Tallmadge's company of dra-goons, all riding back and forth to stem the tide of retreat. At the height of the battle, Lafayette was shot from his horse, taking a bullet in the upper leg. His courage under fire won the admiration of the general and the rest of the staff, includ-ing his friends Hamilton and Laurens.

In time, the Americans got themselves reorganized, com-pany by company, regiment by regiment, and, in good order, they left the enemy in possession of the field. The British did not pursue them with any enthusiasm. After the fighting wound down, Hamilton found a stray dog coming into the American lines. On the collar was the name of its owner.

Taking the time to write a note on behalf of his commander-in-chief, Hamilton sent it and the dog through the lines under a flag of truce:

> General Washington's compliments to General Howe. He does himself the pleasure to return him a dog which accidentally fell into our hands, and by the inscription on the collar appears to belong to General Howe.

After the battle, as the rebels reorganized, shouldered arms, and withdrew, they were heard again and again to say they would do better next time.

*T*HAT NEXT TIME ALMOST CAME a few days later, when the audacious Washington massed his force for an attack on Howe's army, which drew up, ready to fight. It appeared that the decisive open-field battle Howe wanted was about to happen.

Reassured by his army's performance at Brandywine, Washington was prepared to gamble everything, when a tremendous summer downpour suddenly swept both armies, soaking the black powder. Unwilling to match bayonet for bayonet, Washington drew his army off again, unable to defend Philadelphia. Congress fled to York, Pennsylvania, where it reassembled, hoping its army would do something at last.

Knox wrote an account of the campaign to Massachusetts officials, saying, "Our army is now refreshed, and, if the enemy advance, will meet them with that intrepid spirit which becomes men contending for liberty and the great cause of their country."

Shaw sent a letter home with a good friend, an artilleryman who had been stabbed eight times in the recent clash at Paoli, where British troops had surprised an American detachment at night and bayoneted scores of men before the rebels escaped. Shaw told his father that "our misfortune at Brandywine occasioned some small depression of spirits in our army" but "the temporary gloom seems to be entirely dispelled, and our camp is as cheerful as ever."

Word of the British victory at Brandywine and the subsequent fall of Philadelphia dismayed the friends of America in Europe. It was not surprising to see the ragtag rebels swept aside, of course, and most thought it a wonder they had been able to remain in the field this long. Then came news from America that was electrifying: In the face of that sound defeat at Brandywine, Washington had gathered his forces and attacked Howe once more.

Early in October, the Americans had caught the bulk of Howe's army in its encampments at Germantown, near Philadelphia, the first assaults driving the startled British before them. Shaw later wrote home that the enemy surprise "could not have been greater had they seen an army drop from the clouds to oppose them." At the critical moment, however, there had been confusion in the American troop dispositions and maneuver. Then a stone house that the redcoats had stubbornly defended in a key central position had slowed the advance, costing time and lives. One of Washington's aides, John Laurens of South Carolina, impetuously joined in the futile charges on the house and was badly wounded. A dense fog had caused even more American confusion, resulting in regiments accidentally firing on each other. Taking advantage of American inexperience, the enemy had been

The Battle of Germantown late in 1777 almost resulted in a rout of the surprised British Army, but inexperience cost the Americans time, ending in another defeat for Washington.

able to rally, then to bring up strong reinforcements from Cornwallis's garrison in Philadelphia and launch a counterattack.

The Americans could almost taste victory, which was so narrowly missed that every soldier knew they had come close to routing Howe and actually destroying his army. Shaw could only conclude that "it was not the will of Heaven that we should succeed, and by one bold push purchase the inestimable blessing of Freedom."

Howe had held the field at Germantown, but once again the Americans had withdrawn in good order, knowing that victory had been at their fingertips and would have been won if only their battlefield maneuvering had been better executed. The army was in sore need of such training. Washington withdrew to winter quarters at Valley Forge, a hill-country encampment within striking distance of Philadelphia, where Howe settled down for the winter.

To the French, the fact that Washington had counterattacked with such success at Germantown was almost as impressive as the astounding news that Burgoyne had been defeated and captured at Saratoga. He fell to the army under Gates—an army led on the battlefield and inspired to victory by Benedict Arnold, although Gates made no mention in official dispatches of Arnold's achievements.

*D*URING THE PENNSYLVANIA CAMPAIGN, royal soldiers and their American prisoners were treated by the same British Army surgeons, who passed along information about the incident in which Washington had encountered the man who had beckoned to him. That man was Major Patrick Ferguson, perhaps the finest ranger leader in Howe's army. A Scot by birth, Ferguson had spent most of his life and military service in America and the Caribbean. He and some British riflemen had been out scouting along the Brandywine, concealed in the woods when Washington passed by, not once, but twice. The first time, Ferguson had whispered for three marksmen to shoot down this impressive-looking rebel officer on the large gray, although he had not realized it was Washington himself. The men took aim, but Ferguson had a revulsion to the idea of shooting an unsuspecting man in the back, and called it off.

Washington had ridden on, unaware he was being watched. Shortly afterward, the general had come riding by again. This time Ferguson thought to capture him by pretending friendship and calling him over. Washington had eyed Ferguson but did not answer, riding onward slowly, calmly. Again, he would have been easy to shoot, particularly because Ferguson and his men carried a special rifle of his own novel design: breech-loading instead of muzzle-loading, and therefore quick to fire. Soon after Washington was out of sight, an American bullet caught Ferguson in the arm and put him out of the battle.

Later, Ferguson told this story to the surgeon tending his wound. The surgeon had just finished dressing the wounds of American prisoners, who had described Washington on his gray horse, riding alone that day except for the escort of a French hussar. Ferguson said, "I could have lodged half-a-dozen of balls in or about him before he was out of my reach." Yet he was not sorry he had spared George Washington, for he considered it "not pleasant to fire at the back of an unoffending individual, who was acquitting himself very coolly of his duty, so I let him alone."

Ferguson returned to the British Army and would die leading loyalist forces in the 1780 rebel victory at King's Mountain in the Carolinas.

MEMORIES AND CONSPIRACY

*N*OTHING HAD PREPARED THEM FOR this moment; nothing could have prepared them to take leave of His Excellency for the last time.

Perhaps if there had been a great victory ball in Philadelphia, a banquet of all the officers and their ladies, everyone glittering and merry—perhaps then the farewell would not have come upon them so suddenly like this, so unexpectedly. Then again, so much of what had been momentous in the war had come upon them unexpectedly, even the peace, announced this autumn almost two years after Yorktown.

Actually, to officers like Colonel Nicholas Fish, almost everything about the war had been unexpected because they were so young. A lad of nineteen could not know what to expect while leading an infantry charge for the first time. At Saratoga, he had found himself out in front of a thousand men, bayonets leveled, howling a battle-cry, rushing a line of British grenadiers, right up to the muzzles of their Brown Bess muskets. Smoke and flame had erupted, but the Americans had charged through it, amid screams, growls, and clashing of bayonets.

All that was done with now. A memory.

What could any soldier really remember about fighting on a day like that? Wreathed in smoke, the air reeking of burned gunpowder, a constant, infernal din of cannon thundering and massed musketry roaring. The grenadiers had fallen back, Fish and his men driving them, some of the best British troops, driving them back, soldier to soldier. It would not be the last time.

In the Long Room was Brigadier-general Philip van Cortlandt, another native of New York City, who had been colonel of the 2nd New York. Van Cortlandt, now thirty-four years of age, had been with Fish and William Hull in the frontal attack that overran the grenadier line at Saratoga. In the following years, those three had led Americans in other remarkable bayonet charges: at Monmouth, Stony Point, Yorktown. To them and all the men in the Long Room, memories of the war, once so fearsome and awesome and astounding, were fading. Nothing had prepared them for that, either.

When they left this room today, the Revolution would be finished. It would live only in memories, such as that unexpected event at the close of the Pennsylvania campaign of 1777, when General Howe had timidly pulled all his troops into Philadelphia. He had wanted them protected behind strong fortifications—and this after winning two battlefield victories over Washington. Howe's worry had been a remarkable testimony to the tough little rebel army lurking in the nearby hills. Over in Paris, when Benjamin Franklin had been told that Howe had captured the capital city of the rebellion, he had replied, "No, Philadelphia has captured Howe!"

The first governor of New York and a delegate to the Continental Congress that declared independence, George Clinton had served in French and Indian War campaigns; during the Revolution he was in command of the defenses of the Hudson Highlands, including the construction of West Point; later, he participated in warfare against Loyalists and Indians raiding the frontier settlements.

Indeed. Would the men in the Long Room remember only such appealing things? Would Hamilton prefer to forget galloping into Philadelphia after the Brandywine defeat, desperate to requisition supplies, but being denied as merchants shook their heads and said they had nothing? Everyone knew the supplies were there, but hidden, awaiting Howe's army with its British money. Would Knox remember the bitterness he read in a letter from Henry Jackson, who had said the fall of Philadelphia to the British might turn out to be a good thing, for it would "break up all our damned money-makers who are making their fortunes on the war in this country"? Would James Clinton long recall the instant he took a bayonet stab to the body on that day in October 1777 when four thousand British regulars stormed Fort Clinton and defeated his five hundred men? Clinton had been saved by the garrison orderly book, which had been in his pocket and deflected the force of the thrust. John Lamb had been there, too, not long after being exchanged and permitted to resume his military service. Lamb had commanded the water batteries in that hopeless but obstinate defense of forts Clinton and Montgomery, and he had survived by fighting his way out, sword in hand, through the encircling enemy. Would he want to remember so bitter a defeat?

Would Richard Varick forget the loud arguments he had witnessed between Benedict Arnold and Horatio Gates, the commander at Saratoga? Arnold had wanted to attack, and the dithering Gates had tried to keep him out of the fight, had even rudely insulted him. Varick, Philip Schuyler's aide back then, had expected a duel between Arnold and Gates, but Arnold had rushed off against orders and been badly wounded in the battle. Would Samuel Webb ever forget being captured in December of that year as he sailed across Long Island Sound, on a raid against enemy positions? Or would his joyous exchange months later always overcome memories of that dismal, humiliating moment of being taken prisoner?

Would Governor George Clinton often think of January 1778, when he could not find provisions and construction material to build the first defensive works on West Point? Impossible as it had seemed at the time, he had found a way to do it, risking his personal funds and credit to erect the most crucial stronghold on Hudson's River. Early in 1778, Baron von Steuben, too, had faced a daunting military task, trying to teach the American soldiers at Valley Forge a uniform system of drill and maneuver—no matter how he shouted and swore at them in French or German. Would he remember that in years to come? Or would he only recall how, in the end, they had made him infinitely proud—as had young Nicholas Fish, the superb young officer who, the Baron had said, would shine in the finest European army?

Fish had his own troubling memories, though more intimate than memories of commanding armies, defending fortresses, winning great victories. He surely would never forget that terrible moment with his distraught father and sister, telling them he could not go into New York to see his mother, could not leave his post, no matter how ill she was. His Excellency had learned about it and had commended him for devotion to duty, but Fish had never seen his mother or father again. Both had died before the coming of peace.

Such heartache and sorrow, the madness and horror of battle, the grueling marches in summer heat that killed strong men—all these things had been unimaginable in the comfortable New York City law office where Nicholas Fish had been a sixteen-year-old clerk the year the war began. A native of the city, Fish had studied a while at the College of New Jersey in Princeton, returning home and joining the "Hearts of Oak" anti-British militia along with Hamilton and Lamb. Their unit's name had come from the title of a popular soldier tune they drilled to on the city Commons. The Hearts of Oak corps had led the 1775 raid to take the guns from Fort George, drawing the cannonade from the HMS *Asia*.

Fish's employer, attorney John Morin Scott, had become his brigade commander in the early battles around New York and in the defense of Hudson's River. Serving in the 2nd New York Regiment, Fish had been Scott's brigade major, the equivalent of a military clerk, just as he had been Scott's law clerk in civilian life. Thus had rebel companies and regiments, brigades and armies, taken shape at first, as friends and neighbors united to resist the rule of Parliament. A community's leading men naturally assumed command, until others rose in rank by ability and courage and luck.

Nicholas Fish was among the very best.

*N*O DOUBT ALEXANDER HAMILTON WOULD always remember the infuriating insolence of General Horatio Gates that autumn of 1777, after Brandywine, Saratoga, and Germantown. Gates refused the commander-in-chief's direct orders to send reinforcements to strengthen the Delaware River forts below Philadelphia. Basking in the glory of commanding at Saratoga, Gates was maneuvering to replace Washington, and he had secret allies in his plots. The truth was that his victory had come largely by reaping what Schuyler had sown, and Gates had been hanging back at headquarters while Arnold led the troops into battle.

It was a gloomy, chill November as Hamilton rode night and day through cold and rain all the way to Albany to convey Washington's orders that Gates send reinforcements before Howe took the forts and opened the Delaware to supply his army in Philadelphia. But Gates put Hamilton off, deliberately delaying reinforcements.

Gates was the idol of the New Englanders, the triumphant general poised to replace the mediocre Washington, who had only the bare survival of his pitifully small army to show for his best efforts. Gates was establishing his position separate from and equal to Washington—an insubordination that was proved when he never officially reported the Saratoga victory to the commander-in-chief, only to Congress, as if Gates were

A native of New York City, Nicholas Fish was one of the finest infantry officers in the Continental Army; he was a brigade inspector for Steuben, and selected by Lafayette to be an officer in an elite light infantry corps established in 1780.

an independent field commander. Further, Gates interfered in petty, insulting ways with officers in his command who were known to be loyal to Washington. This included John Lamb, whose artillery units in the valley of Hudson's River were never permitted to be consolidated under him but were scattered under the local command of officers junior to Lamb. Again and again Lamb had to fight Gates's moves to give lower-ranking officers prerogatives and authority that undercut Lamb's.

From a close friend who served on Gates's staff, Hamilton learned about the correspondence between Gates and his cohorts in Congress and the army. The whisperers said Washington was a sincere man but a weak general who listened too much to "bad counselors." Those counselors were Knox, Greene, and Hamilton. The ambitious Gates was also secretly corresponding with another scheming general: Thomas Conway, a Frenchman of Irish descent, and with extensive command experience in the French service. Conway had done well leading a division of troops at Germantown, but he possessed a high opinion of himself and a low one of Washington. When the commander-in-chief learned about the conspiratorial nature of this correspondence, he confronted both Gates and Conway, both of whom denied any intent other than to express privately their frank opinions of the war situation. Both men had their backers in Congress and the army, and controversy swirled among the staff as the troops built huts against the approach of winter at the Valley Forge refuge.

John Adams of Massachusetts was particularly fond of Gates, and apparently saw a silver lining in Washington's defeats outside Philadelphia. Adams wrote home that he was glad Gates, not Washington, had earned the glory of defeating Burgoyne, for had Washington been the victor, then "idolatry and adulation would have been unbounded, so excessive as to endanger our liberties." Adams feared—or perhaps was simply jealous of—Washington's high standing with the troops and the people at large. The rise of Horatio Gates would diminish Washington and prevent his establishing a military dictatorship to replace British rule.

In the winter months of 1778, with Howe's army warm in Philadelphia and the Americans suffering from hunger and cold at Valley Forge, a number of politicians and generals thought either Conway or Gates should take Washington's place as commander-in-chief, and the whispering campaign intensified.

*W*OULD THE OFFICERS IN THE LONG ROOM in 1783 remember the Conway Cabal, as the conspiracy was termed? Gates might as well have lent his own name to it, but he had been more slippery than the high-strung Conway, who had bluntly spoken up and asserted to Congress that he deserved higher rank than virtually all the other generals. He had offered to resign if not satisfied. At one point, Washington, too, had threatened to resign if Congress persisted with its plans to promote Conway over more deserving generals, who would certainly leave the army themselves if the Frenchman were given higher rank.

Washington wrote, "I have undergone more than most men are aware of to harmonize so many discordant parts; but it will be impossible for me to be of any further service if such insuperable difficulties are thrown in my way."

Even Washington's enemies in Congress could not condone the petulant Conway's repeated insults of American officers, and he became an embarrassment to Gates and Adams. Eventually, Conway's resignation had been accepted—much to his own surprise, for he had been bluffing.

Was there really a genuine cabal against Washington? Hamilton and Lafayette, other aides, and several general officers were sure of it. Everyone in the army seemed to have heard the slander against Washington, of his being the pliant victim of bad counselors.

That winter, Gates came down to York from Albany and, with the collaboration of his admirers, was named by Congress as president of the newly formed Board of War, which meant he shared with the board direct authority over

Washington and military operations. Yet, even though some of Congress's delegates from New England and Pennsylvania favored Gates, he found himself permanently outside the circle of the commander-in-chief's confidantes and would never break Washington's hold on the faithful army.

VALLEY FORGE AND THE BARON

*T*HE TROUBLE BETWEEN WASHINGTON AND GATES was well-known to Baron von Steuben when first he arrived at York early in February 1778. He had been told about it by John Hancock, former president of Congress, on a visit to Boston a few weeks earlier. Steuben intended to keep out of the controversy, and so declined Gates's invitation to be his house-guest while staying at York. Instead, the Baron took up residence in a mansion there that belonged to Hancock.

Baron Friedrich Wilhelm Augustus von Steuben had come from Prussia, via Paris, to join Washington's army as a volunteer without an officer's commission. He was willing to accept whatever duty the commander-in-chief deemed fitting, and specifically was prepared to train soldiers in the much-admired system of his former patron, Frederick the Great of Prussia, the most illustrious general of the age. Benjamin Franklin had sent Washington a letter of introduction that exaggerated Steuben's military status, describing him as "Lieut. Genl. in the king of Prussia's service, whom he attended in all his campaigns, being his aid de camp, quartermaster

Genl., etc." The truth was that Steuben had never been a
Prussian general officer at all, and the implication that he was
still in service with Frederick was a blatant fabrication.

It is likely that Franklin was the one who also drafted a
modest letter in English to Congress, signed by Steuben,
and requesting "The honor of serving a respectable Nation,
engaged in the noble enterprize of defending its rights and
liberty," adding that this was the "only motive that brought
me over to this Continent." The cunningly crafted letter of
introduction to the Continental Congress was needed, in
part, to overcome American objections to yet another foreign officer appearing before them and demanding high
rank in the army.

By now, Congress had suffered too many incompetent,
supercilious European gentlemen soldiers, and Franklin had
been told to send them no more. The wise old statesman
knew, however, that Steuben was the man to organize and
train the Americans. Thus, he concocted a false reputation for
Baron von Steuben, who, if not a qualified lieutenant-general
experienced in the field, possessed the ability to impart the
basic techniques of Prussian drill.

Franklin's introduction caused Congress to warmly welcome so distinguished a volunteer, and at first Steuben was
addressed as "Your Excellency," an honorific to which he had
no claim. No one challenged the remarkable credentials
Franklin had conferred upon him, and Steuben did not
admit that he had served only in the quartermaster (supply)
department. Actually, one of the shortcomings of
Washington's army was poor organization in the quartermaster department, which desperately needed an experienced
executive officer. Steuben's personal interest, however, was

leading men into action as a field general. First, the army had to survive the winter.

*A*T THE HEART OF THE FAILURE OF military supply at Valley Forge was the policy of Congress that each state was obliged to provide for its own regiments. Most of the states were not competent to carry out the complex and expensive task of supplying soldiers at such a distant cantonment. Some states tangled up the endeavor by appointing slow-moving committees, or simply were unable to find the funds or credit to buy and ship what was needed.

Bureaucracy and politics in home states deeply frustrated Washington, who accused the politicians of enjoying "a comfortable room by a good fireside" while their troops had to "occupy a bleak hill and sleep under frost and snow without clothes or blankets." The average soldier at Valley Forge could not afford to buy from local farmers because the army had not been paid for five months. Making things worse, Washington's previous quartermaster general—who was a secret conspirator in the whispering campaign—had resigned to take a post on the Board of War, which had several members, including Gates, who were trouble to the general. One member of the board had been heard to remark that if the men had no meat or vegetables, they should substitute bread. For a time, there was no bread to be had, either.

To keep warm, men lacking blankets sat up by fires all night instead of sleeping in beds; many were confined to hospitals for want of shoes; others had little more than a blanket to wear and so were unable to stand guard or do routine camp duties; still others were dying daily from exposure and

There was little to eat and not much shelter in the first weeks Washington's army was at Valley Forge after the British captured Philadelphia; here he is pictured with Lafayette.

hunger that weakened them. Two thousand men from an army of fewer than nine thousand at Valley Forge would be buried there.

Yet the troops stood by Washington, once even sending a delegation to assure him they understood his difficulties. The general was left in tears by the "patience and fidelity of the soldiery."

"What is to become of the army this winter?" he wrote to Henry Laurens, president of Congress, who was an ally. "This army must inevitably be reduced to one or the other of three things. Starve, dissolve, or disperse, in order to obtain subsistence in the best manner they can...."

The general had no intention of giving up and leaving the army, however, as was proved when Martha came from Mount Vernon that February to join him once more. This isolated winter cantonment offered hardly any compatible society for a lady of breeding, with not much company other than the headquarters staff. Yet they were charming and faithful, those gallant young aides, and upon her arrival they somehow rounded up a few bottles of wine, some tea, a bit of cheese, bread, and nuts.

Washington's solution to the lack of provisions and equipment was to appoint the dependable, resourceful General Nathanael Greene as quartermaster general. Greene found the supply department in complete disarray. For example, hundreds of forgotten tents were found stored in distant barns; no carts were available to haul what supplies there were in other military depots; and no forage had been procured for draft animals or cavalry horses, which had begun to die of starvation.

Congress could not pay, so it authorized Washington to

take what he needed at bayonet point. That he hated to do, but before the winter was over, he had no other choice but to force farmers to sell him food and forage. Greene was a whirlwind of efficiency, and by mid-February 1778, when Baron Steuben first came to the Valley Forge cantonment, most of the supply problems had been overcome, although clothing was still lacking.

Breeches were especially difficult to come by.

Shortly after arriving at Valley Forge, Steuben had his aides organize a boisterous party at his quarters, with everyone clubbing their rations of food and rum, and no one allowed in who had breeches and stockings that were not torn.

Despite the winter poverty of the soldiers at Valley Forge, their half-naked legs and feet, and their bitterness at war profiteers and politicians, the men were eager to learn from Steuben. In his mid-forties, the Baron cut an impressive military figure, especially on horseback, and one young private described him as "a perfect personification of Mars," the god of war.

The Baron asked Washington for a hundred good men to shape into a "model company" that would be the example for the rest of the army. These men would, in their turn, impart his Prussian-style training to the others. Nicholas Fish and William Hull were in this select group, and they became two of the Baron's favorites, eventually to be appointed division inspectors responsible for overseeing the training of hundreds of men in several regiments. Hull, in particular, was so apt a pupil that in time he became Steuben's first assistant inspector.

*S*TEUBEN SPOKE GERMAN AND FRENCH, but no English at first, except for the word "Goddamn!" which came in handy as he began to drill his hundred picked men. Yet, one swear word was not much for a drillmaster. His own aide, a French gentleman who had come with him to America, knew English well enough, but was not an experienced military man able to understand or issue drill commands properly. The result often was comic confusion.

With Azor, his rangy Italian greyhound, tagging along behind, the Baron attempted with sign language to show what he wanted the men to do. This only caused the model company to become all the more disordered, and as his face turned red, Steuben sputtered curses in German and in French, well peppered with his "Goddamn!" All the while, the hundreds of soldiers looking on at the edge of the parade ground laughed to see some men turning this way, others blundering that way.

At length, as the Baron again exploded in helpless rage, a young captain stepped out of the crowd of spectators and addressed him in French, saying he would be honored to be of assistance. This was Benjamin Walker, who had been born in England and emigrated to New York City, where he had become a successful merchant before the war, though only in his early twenties. He had joined the 2nd New York Regiment and had earned a reputation as an excellent officer. Steuben accepted his offer and gave the next command. Walker shouted it out with the authority of a veteran, and the men responded correctly. Steuben was impressed. More commands with precise translations, and the model company began to look promising.

The Baron thought Walker an angel from heaven. Not that the drilling and marching always went perfectly at first, but the men improved swiftly. Whenever they failed, and the German or French curses did no good, Steuben called on Walker to swear at them in English.

The troops liked the Prussian from the start, especially because in this day no officer ever drilled common soldiers. Training men was beneath the officer's station and was instead the duty of experienced sergeants, which the British Army had in abundance but the Americans sorely lacked. Moreover, the Baron was believed to be a Prussian lieutenant-general, and if he condescended to train men day after day, through the mud and cold and wet of winter, then other officers would gladly learn to do the same.

Working hard for Steuben, the model company steadily improved, and the spectators no longer laughed, for they were too busy trying to grasp the maneuvers themselves, many learning the rudiments by watching the daily exercises. Their chance would come next. Once the basic manual of arms, including bayonet practice, was thoroughly learned, the men were taught those movements essential to effective, rapid maneuvering in battle formations. The Baron taught them to march in columns of four abreast rather than in single file— "Indian-style," favored by militia companies used to forest trails—and from four abreast to deploy as a unit into line of battle. Deploying into line from four abreast was four times as rapid as deploying from a single file. The defeats at Brandywine and Germantown had both been largely attributable to slow deployment and lack of training in large-unit maneuvering.

Now the troops learned to wheel and turn in small units

of ten men, then in companies of twenty-five, and then as a unit of one hundred. When the model company was deemed ready, its members dispersed back into their regiments to train the rank and file, which eagerly listened and learned. Some of the general officers felt Steuben was impinging on their authority, and they grumbled that it was the responsibility of each state to train its troops as it saw fit. Washington smoothed over their objections, and in time, all Valley Forge was alive with hard-working soldiers marching back and forth across regimental parades. When not drilling their own regiments, the men of the model company continued to be trained by Steuben at more complex maneuvers. The model company stayed a few lessons ahead of the army as a whole.

The Baron wrote with pride to a friend: "My enterprize succeeded better than I had dared to expect, and I had the satisfaction, in a month's time, to see not only a regular step introduced in the army, but I also made maneuvers with ten and twelve battalions with as much precision as the evolution of a single company."

Training independent-minded Americans was a totally new experience to Steuben, who was used to the average peasant soldier responding to an officer with immediate obedience. Steuben wrote to his friend that Prussians, Austrians, and French officers say to the soldier, "'Do this,' and he does it, but I am obliged to say 'This is the reason why you ought to do that,' and then he does it."

Washington could not have been more pleased with the Baron, who by sheer determination, and thanks to his faith in the Americans, was working what became known as the "Miracle of Valley Forge." Not only could the men march well in formations of companies, regiments, and brigades, but

A Prussian officer in the quartermaster corps, Friedrich Wilhelm von Steuben came to America in 1778 with the encouragement of French officials; he was instrumental in training Washington's troops at Valley Forge.

there was a newfound confidence in the bayonet. Once the dreaded weapon only of the redcoats, and seldom used by Americans except as a skewer for cooking meat, the bayonet became lethal in the Continental soldier's hands. By springtime, he was eager to use it in battle.

$\mathcal{O}$n May 6, 1778, the Continentals at Valley Forge had the opportunity to show how well they could march, as Washington announced a celebration to commemorate the stupendous news that France had allied herself with America against the British. Now there was hope for ultimate victory as never before.

The Baron took charge of the parade and the "fire of joy"

that was the climax of the celebrations. Young John Laurens, who had recovered from the wound inflicted at Germantown, wrote proudly to his father, the president of Congress, about that joyous day:

> Divine service preceded the rejoicing. After a proper pause, the several brigades marched by their right to their posts in order of battle, and the line was formed with admirable rapidity and precision. Three salutes of artillery, thirteen each, and three general discharges of a running fire by the musquetry were given in honor of the King of France, the friendly European powers, and the United American States.

In this "running fire," or "fire of joy," each soldier fired into the air in succession, the discharges running down the length of ranks two deep, and then back down the length of parallel ranks. Laurens, who with Hamilton had done much to help Steuben become established with the army, described it:

> The order with which the whole was conducted, the beautiful effect of the running fire which was executed to perfection, the martial appearance of the troops, gave sensible pleasure to everyone present.

The event was all the more satisfying because many officers' ladies as well as prominent civilian guests were in attendance to see the army's new achievements. Laurens wrote his father about the buffet afterward, a "cold collation" for officers and guests; he said that Washington, whom he so admired, received such proofs of the love and attachment of his officers as must have given him the most exquisite feelings. If ever there was a man in the world whose moderation and patriotism fitted him for the command of a Republican army, he is, and he merits unrestrained confidence....

So, too, did Baron Steuben merit America's confidence that day. Thus, General Washington took great personal pleasure in announcing before the guests at the banquet that his volunteer drillmaster had been appointed to the position of Inspector General, with the rank and pay of a major general, in charge of all training in the army.

Regarding how Washington and the army felt at the celebration of the French alliance, the commander-in-chief wrote, "I believe no event was ever received with more heartfelt joy."

The heart of Nicholas Fish, too, was full of joy at what they had achieved, and full with new hope for the Revolution. Fish's happiness was soon tempered, though, for this was when he received a letter from his sister, Sally, telling that his mother had died.

Fish wrote to his good friend, Lieutenant-colonel Richard Varick, who was in New York: "I am taught the useful lesson of mortality and to know how closely the miseries of this life are allied with its pleasures." He regretted that during his mother's illness his "absence gave her infinite distress." Still, he believed in the "propriety of my conduct, which was founded upon the pure principles of duty and love to my country."

Devotion to duty, essential to a superb officer, had its price.

*T*HE OUTLOOK WAS BRIGHT for the coming campaign, and the army was increasingly robust. High spirits went along with good training, and Washington enjoyed the warm, fine days of springtime. He played ball with his officers, and even did his men "the honor to play at wicket," as cricket was called.

Connecticut surgeon Albigence Waldo, a twenty-seven-year-old wit, artist, and musician, composed verse at Valley Forge, some of it expressing how optimistic the soldiers felt, largely thanks to their training:

> *The day serene—joy sparkles round*
> *Camp, hills and dales with mirth resound,*
> *All with clean clothes and powder'd hair*
> *For sport or duty now appear,*
> *Here squads in martial exercise,*
> *There whole brigades in order rise,*
> *With cautious steps they march and wheel.*
> *Double—form ranks—platoons—at will.*
> *Columns on columns justly roll,*
> *Advance, retreat, or form one whole.*

Spirits rose even higher when news arrived that General Howe had resigned in humiliation for failure to defeat the rebellion. Howe was replaced by his second-in-command, Sir Henry Clinton, headquartered in New York City. Further, spies reported the stirring news that the British were preparing to abandon Philadelphia altogether. If the royal army marched overland to New York, it would be strung out for many miles, vulnerable to attack and piecemeal defeat.

In mid-May, Steuben's training was tested in the field when, with about twenty-eight hundred men, Lafayette took up a position near Philadelphia. The Marquis's presence was discovered by the enemy, who secretly sent three strong columns on forced marches to surround the detachment before it could escape. The British expected the rebel army to be as unwieldy and slow to maneuver as ever. So confident were they that Lafayette was doomed that Howe delayed his departure from the city and planned a dinner to which "the Boy," as they called Lafayette, would be brought as guest of honor.

Instead, Lafayette learned of the danger, assembled his men, and moved swiftly out of trouble. The British were amazed to find themselves for the first time outmarched by Americans.

MONMOUTH AND BEYOND

*T*HE NEXT DAY, MAJOR GENERAL Charles Lee returned to Washington's army. Since late 1776, Lee had been a prisoner of war in New York, and later in Philadelphia, allowed the freedom of the city on his promise not to try to escape. He had been exchanged recently for a British officer of comparable stature.

Though still as unkempt, rude, and foulmouthed as ever, Lee was rightfully second-in-command to Washington, who deferred to protocol and welcomed him back to full rank.

Virtually all the Americans considered Lee a great soldier and a welcome addition to the rejuvenated army—at least at first. From the start, he disparaged the new drill methods, sneered at Prussian techniques—which he had never learned in his career as a professional soldier in Europe. Nor did he understand them. Lee haughtily told his friends that the army "had gone to the dogs" in his absence. One member of Congress reported to a friend that Lee said he had "found the army in worse condition than he expected, and that General Washington was not fit to command a sergeant's guard."

In mid-June, the British Army left Philadelphia, its great column of supply wagons snaking slowly across New Jersey toward New York City. General Washington called a council of war. He wanted to attack Clinton, but many of his officers were hesitant when Charles Lee warned against it, saying Americans were no match for regulars. Lee insisted it was best to let the enemy go back to New York—to give them "a golden bridge" that would prove the Americans wanted peace and reconciliation with Britain, an end to the war. Now that the French alliance was certain, it was wise, he said, to let the power of France come to bear rather than hurl inept American troops onto British bayonets. Lee convinced the majority of the officers, and Washington accepted the council's decision not to launch a full-scale attack on the enemy column.

That evening, the agitated Greene, Steuben, and Lafayette sent messages to Washington, asking him to reconsider, pleading with him to attack. In truth, he wanted to attack, but felt bound by the council of war and by Lee's warnings. As a compromise, Washington sent a strong force under Lafayette to strike at the enemy's supply train near the rear of the column.

*O*NCE IT HAD BECOME APPARENT THAT Washington intended to bring on a heavy clash with the rear of the British column, Lee requested command of the advance troops instead of Lafayette, whose force had been steadily increased as the movement developed from probing raid to impending all-out battle.

In the sultry heat of the mosquito-ridden Jersey lowlands in early summer, Nicholas Fish marched in the command of General Anthony Wayne. "Mad Anthony," they called him, for his unrelenting urge to attack, no matter what. Men were dropping from heat stroke. It had to be even worse for the redcoats in their full uniforms and heavy marching kits. Wayne's force, in Lee's division of five thousand select troops, was approaching the enemy column, but without much in the way of clear orders from Lee. So it was with each unit of Americans; they were eager to attack, but unsure what they were expected to do. When orders did come from Lee, too often they were soon countermanded, causing confusion in the advance troops. Lee was nowhere in sight of Wayne's command when they saw about a thousand of the enemy's rear guard forming up.

This British force was several miles distant from its main body, and therefore vulnerable. Wayne led his men toward them with the bayonet. The clash drove the outnumbered redcoats back, but a larger enemy force was coming up. Wayne took defensive positions and sent to Lee for reinforcements. Suddenly there came the thunder of British dragoons charging down on the surprised Americans. Near White Plains in the New York campaign these very same dragoons had crashed into the American ranks, scattering them like chaff. They meant to do it again.

Wayne formed his men in firing lines. Closer came the cavalry, plumed leather helmets shining in the sun, swords raking above their heads, riding down on the American infantry. These were the 16th Light Dragoons, the "Queen's Own," the regiment raised by John Burgoyne—Lee's former regiment, the one that had captured him in 1776.

Nicholas Fish and his troops coolly waited, aimed, and on command opened fire, dropping men and horses to the ground. They did not give an inch, fighting as Mad Anthony demanded they fight, as the Baron had taught them to fight. The dragoons were shattered, many troopers littering the field, riderless horses galloping back and forth. The surviving horsemen turned and fled all the way back to the safety of their infantry.

Wayne reassembled his men, collected the wounded, and prepared for the fight to go on. Then he realized that his force was alone, without American support on either side. The enemy was preparing to counterattack as powerful reinforcements and artillery came hurrying up. Wayne ordered a withdrawal, taking his artillery with him, and wondering what had happened to the rest of the army. Too late, he learned that Lee had ordered a general retreat, but had not sent word to him.

Far to the rear, George Washington was galloping full speed on his magnificent white horse toward the battle. He was dismayed to see swarms of Lee's men glumly trudging away from the front and declaring that the enemy were after them.

Finding Lee casually riding along with some aides, Washington dashed up to him, reined in his mount, and shouted, "What is the meaning of this?"

"Sir? Sir?"

"What is all this confusion for, and retreat?" Washington could not restrain his fury.

Lee expected praise from the general for extricating the command, and he blurted out, "Sir, these troops are not able to meet British grenadiers."

"Sir! They are able!" Washington bellowed. "And by God, they shall do it!"

The general ordered Lee to the rear and took charge of the army, his very presence stopping the retreat. Riding back and forth, forming firing lines, stationing cannon, he was cheered and shouted to by the adoring soldiers.

Lafayette later said, "I thought then…never had I beheld so superb a man."

Hamilton remembered, "I never saw the general to so much advantage. His coolness and firmness were admirable. He instantly took measures for checking the enemy's advance…."

Wayne and Fish came in with their powder-blackened, do-or-die comrades, the British following close behind. Henry Jackson was there with his regiment, having come up from Philadelphia where he had commanded the force that first reoccupied the city. Knox and Shaw were ready with cannon, stopping the British in their tracks, blasting away in a duel with the enemy artillery, and outgunning them. The British would praise Knox's artillery at Monmouth as being equal to their own. Knox galloped all over the field, directing placement of his guns, trying to take the enemy from the flank. In one bizarre instance, a cannonball fired down a line of British troops knocked the muskets out of the hands of an entire platoon.

Washington gallops up to prevent Charles Lee, left of center, from allowing his army to retreat at the Battle of Monmouth, which was a successful engagement for the Americans, although the British defended their supply train.

John Hays, one of Knox's cannoneers, collapsed from the heat, and his wife, Molly, who had been carrying water to the men and tending the wounded, threw aside her pitcher and took his place at the gun for the rest of the battle.

Steuben and Walker were in the thick of it after reconnoitering for Washington and narrowly escaping capture by some enemy dragoons. The horsemen had been ordered by Knyphausen to take the Baron alive, although they had the chance to shoot him down. He galloped away, leaping a fence, and losing his fine hat in the dash to American lines. When he approached the battlefield and saw his trainees advancing "with as much precision as on ordinary parade," Steuben was thrilled.

William Hull and Benjamin Tallmadge were there that fiercely hot day, when it was later said the regular American army was born. So many fought gallantly, and none better than Hamilton, who was at Washington's beck and call, his heroics winning him fame as he rode around the battlefield with the general's orders to the commanders, rallying soldiers to stand against a powerful charge, and falling, unhurt, when his horse was shot under him.

Black Watch, British and Hessian grenadiers, Guards, light infantry—the best soldiers Clinton possessed—stormed the American lines, thinking this was the chance they had been after to destroy Washington at last. Attack and counterattack, the battle raged, with the Americans giving as good as they got, and maneuvering skillfully against the British attempts to turn their line or to find a crack in the defenses. At the very end of the sweltering, bloody day, British grenadiers made a last headlong rush at the center of Wayne's line, and they were stopped, their lieutenant-colonel falling dead at the feet of the Americans.

Clinton broke off the attack in good order. He had pro-tected his wagon train, which escaped capture, and his force camped in their positions that night. If he had not slipped away before dawn, the Americans would have attacked again. Was it a victory for Washington that day or a successful rear-guard action by Clinton? One tough British veteran of the American war said the royal troops had never been more roughly handled than at Monmouth. Lee's misbehavior had lost the chance of a smashing victory. He would be court-mar-tialed, with Hamilton as a key witness against him, testifying that Lee seemed to be "in a hurry of mind" during the early part of the battle, and that much of his command was in a "settled durable panic" when Washington raced up. Lee would be suspended from command for one year, but would not return to the army.

*C*HARLES LEE WOULD NEVER HAVE COME to the farewell in the Long Room, if he had still lived, for he had proved himself Washington's nemesis that brutally hot New Jersey day in June 1778. The army had been ready and willing to attack, but it was clear that Lee had no faith in it. How could he? Lee had not been there from the rally and counterattack at Trenton to the training at Valley Forge.

After the Battle of Monmouth, Lee had been disgraced, banished from the army, and had died friendless in Philadelphia. General Lee, who had served bravely under Burgoyne in those glorious 16th Dragoon charges against the

Spanish in Portugal in the 1760s, had been a mercenary major-general for the king of Poland, had lost two fingers in a duel in Italy, and since his American service in the French and Indian War had been known to the Mohawks as "Boiling Water," for his ungoverned temper. Charles Lee had proven such an able commander at the start of the war, well deserving the rank next to Washington. Then, after the New York defeats, Lee had begun maneuvering to replace the Virginian and had written to Gates, belittling Washington's ability.

It was rumored that when Lee was a British captive he had been so arrogant as to prepare a plan of campaign whereby the enemy could defeat Washington. Some thought that Howe's move up the Chesapeake against Philadelphia was inspired by Lee's after-dinner scheming with British officers.

There was no Charles Lee in the Long Room in 1783, nor John Laurens. After Monmouth, the youthful aide-de-camp to Washington had been so indignant at Lee's publicly insulting the commander-in-chief that he had challenged the man to a duel with pistols. Hamilton had served as his friend's second. Laurens had wounded Lee in the side, though not fatally. And there was Lee afterwards, cackling about it like the mad gallant he was, declaring how proud John Laurens had made him: "I could have hugged the noble boy, he pleased me so!"

Lee had called Hamilton, who testified at his court-martial, a "son of a bitch," saying Hamilton lied about what happened that day. Hamilton had been there, throughout it all, as Washington's messenger with orders for Lee to attack.

*A*FTER THE BATTLE OF MONMOUTH, CONGRESS had returned to liberated Philadelphia, finding the city filthy and torn up by the occupying army, just as New York would be at the end of the war. Major-general Benedict Arnold assumed command at Philadelphia, soon coming into conflict with his former opponents who favored Gates. There, Arnold married Peggy Shippen, the beautiful daughter of a wealthy Tory, which placed him further at odds with hostile factions in Congress and on the Board of War.

Full-scale action in the war was suspended for many months to follow, although Washington's main force took positions near New York, threatening an attack, ever his dream and cherished hope. A major engagement almost developed later that summer of 1778, when the first French fleet and expeditionary force appeared off the coast. An attempt was made to coordinate operations with an American army against British positions at Newport, Rhode Island, but a vicious storm destroyed the endeavor, damaging ships and breaking up the fleet, which had to find safe harbors for refitting.

It was not until May 1779 that the next significant move developed in the north, as Sir Henry Clinton sent a powerful force up Hudson's River to capture two American-held strongpoints—Stony Point and Verplanck's, about thirty-five miles above the city. The British were successful, but less than two months later, Anthony Wayne retaliated. With William Hull and Benjamin Tallmadge serving under him, Wayne led thirteen hundred picked men on a secret march through mountainous defiles at night. Then, without firing, using only the bayonet, they stormed Stony Point in the darkness.

Tallmadge wrote about that assault under heavy fire from the defenders: "Such was the ardor and impetuosity of the Americans, that they surmounted all difficulties, removed all obstructions, cut away the abatis and a double stockade, mounted the ramparts, and captured the whole garrison in a short time with the bayonet alone."

The bayonet was now an American weapon.

That same year, Nicholas Fish took part in a campaign against the British-allied Iroquois League, which had been raiding New York frontier settlements. The approach of this army forced most of the Iroquois to flee from their villages, abandoning fields, crops, and orchards to destruction. Their houses—many of them finer than anything the soldiers knew at home—were burned down. The Iroquois campaign ended without any real fighting, but it was considered a triumph for breaking the power of the warriors.

A consummate soldier, veteran, and proven commander of fighting men, Fish was just twenty-one years of age at the close of 1779. Soon after, he received another sad letter from his sister Sally, informing him that their father had died suddenly.

$\mathcal{A}$ROUND THIS TIME, NICHOLAS FISH'S FRIEND, Lieutenant-colonel Richard Varick, resolved to leave the army after having served ably in the headquarters of the Northern Department. His patron and former commander, Philip Schuyler, had resigned by now but remained a key advisor to Washington. Elected as a delegate to Congress in 1779, Schuyler served as chairman of a committee at headquarters that had reorganized the army's staff and also coordinated relations with the French forces that were steadily arriving on the New England coast.

Like Fish, Varick had been employed in the New York City law office of John Morin Scott before the war; he had enlisted as a captain in the 1st New York, the regiment of another mutual friend, Alexander McDougall. A native of New Jersey, Varick had just turned twenty-seven when he was requested in the spring of 1780 to come back from his family home in Hackensack, New Jersey, and be aide-de-camp for Benedict Arnold, who was taking command of the works at West Point. Arnold and Varick were well-acquainted. Varick had served him with remarkable effectiveness during the northern campaigns of 1776-77, and with Schuyler's support had worked tirelessly to find the materials needed for Arnold to build the fleet on Lake Champlain, preventing the British from taking control of the lake until the following year. As Schuyler's former secretary, Varick often had come in contact with Arnold during the conflict with Gates, and had formed a high opinion of Arnold. After the Saratoga battle of September 19, 1777, Varick had written to Schuyler: "This I am certain of, that Arnold has all the credit of the action on the 19th, for he was ordering our troops to it, while the other [Gates] was in Dr. Pott's tent backbiting his neighbors."

Varick agreed to come out of his brief retirement, honored to serve so excellent a commander as Arnold at such a crucial place as West Point. Developed and fortified at great expense to Congress, West Point commanded the inland crossroads of supply and reinforcement from New England. An enemy force there would constantly threaten those states with invasion.

The spring and summer of 1780 were as precarious as ever for the rebellion, with the main British operations shifted to the South. Though the population of the South was comparatively small, there was a higher proportion of loyalists, many of whom were fighting men from the back country, more used to handling firearms than were the loyalists of the North, who were usually from the wealthier families and the business class. Savannah, Georgia, was in British hands, and an attempt by General Benjamin Lincoln the previous September to recapture it in concert with a French fleet and invasion force had been resoundingly defeated.

In May, Charleston had fallen to the British, led by Clinton himself, who once again had defeated the outnumbered Lincoln. The British effort to control the South was clearly succeeding by the time the skillful Lord Cornwallis took command from Clinton, who returned to New York in June. Clinton was understandably concerned about Washington, who he feared might be devising some daring plan with the French to attack the city. The country all about New York and northern New Jersey was a no-man's-land, with thousands of partisan fighters and criminal bandits raiding and counter-raiding, stealing, and murdering. That lawless region screened each army from the other, and through it the other might launch a surprise attack in force.

To oppose Cornwallis in the South, Congress put Horatio Gates in charge of an army there. With the laurels from Saratoga still green, Gates gathered a force roughly equal to Cornwallis's, and while hoping for a militia rising in his favor, he maneuvered toward a decisive battle.

*T*HE SPRING OF 1780 WAS ESPECIALLY MEMORABLE for at least one officer in the Fraunces Tavern Long Room, for that was when Lieutenant-colonel David Humphreys had first met His Excellency.

At the time, John Laurens had been an enemy prisoner, captured at the fall of Charleston, and that had left an opening on Washington's staff. To fill it, Humphreys had come from his station in New England, bringing with him the reputation of a proven combat officer and an able brigade major. Yet another Yale graduate from Connecticut, Humphreys had been a lifelong friend of Hull and Tallmadge. Hull, in fact, had first been offered the aide's position, but had declined it and recommended Humphreys instead.

By the end of the war, Humphreys had become one of Washington's closest aides, a man who knew the general's thoughts and style so well that he spared His Excellency the many burdens of writing official correspondence and public addresses. An admired scholar, and well-known as a teacher, Humphreys was often inspired to write verse. While lying in camp near New York City in the disastrous campaign of 1776, he had written a poem in honor of Washington and sent it to the general via another friend, Samuel Webb, then an aide at headquarters. This likely was the first time Humphreys had come to Washington's attention.

Handsome, heroic, and romantic, David Humphreys was twenty-seven that June of 1780, the heartthrob of many a young lady, one of whom, at Boston, received the following verse from him around this time:

The cannon's distant thunders ring,
  And wake to deeds of death the spring:
Far other sounds once touched my ear,
  And ushered in the flow'ry year:
But, now, adieu the tuneful train,
  The warblings of my native plain;
Adieu the scenes that charm'd my view,
  And thou, fair maid, again adieu.

The patriot poet bids farewell, for he is going where "the battle bleeds."

To-morrow—(brief then be my story)—
  I go to WASHINGTON and GLORY;
His aid-de-camp—in acts when tried—
  Resolv'd (whatever fates betide)
My conduct, till my final breath,
  Shall not disgrace my life or death.

Like Baron von Steuben and Benjamin Walker, Humphreys would be traveling on with His Excellency from New York to Annapolis after saying farewell to the others.

TREASON AND WASHINGTON'S LUCK

*T*HERE WAS NO QUESTION, WHEN ONE LOOKED back at the war from the perspective of the Fraunces Tavern Long Room in 1783, that despite all the adversity, His Excellency had been blessed with astonishingly good luck. The fog covering the escape from Long Island, his invulnerability under fire at Princeton and Monmouth, the decision of Ferguson not to kill him at Brandywine, the rainstorm that avoided an unequal battle afterward, the fortunate arrival of Lafayette and Steuben at a time when Congress wanted no more foreign officers, his timely arrival to prevent Lee's retreat at Monmouth…

During the French and Indian War, the Indians had thought Washington led a charmed life. One had shot at him pointblank and missed, and later the Virginian had survived, unscathed, Braddock's bloody defeat near Fort Duquesne. (Horatio Gates, then a young captain, had been wounded there.) Perhaps His Excellency's was, indeed, a charmed and divinely protected life, as many of his soldiers believed, including Samuel Shaw, who wrote home about it to a friend:

"When I contemplate the virtues of the man, uniting the citizen and soldier," Shaw wrote, recalling a recent speaker he had heard, "I cannot too heartily coincide with the orator… who so delicately describes him, as a person that appears to

A Jerseyman of Dutch ancestry, Richard Varick, an officer from the 1st New York, served on Philip Schuyler's staff, later was an aide of Benedict Arnold, and by the end of the war had copied all Washington's official correspondence into bound books.

be raised by Heaven to show how high humanity can soar."

Divine protection? Luck? Coincidence? Which of these—or perhaps all of them—brought Washington to West Point on September 23, 1780? For that was the very moment Benedict Arnold sent vital information on the defenses of West Point to the British. The night before, Arnold had met secretly with Major John Andre to pass on intelligence that could cause the surrender of the post under his command. Arnold was sick of Congress, disgusted with being passed over for promotion, sick of being insulted by politicians and bureaucrats. Now he meant to profit from what he had to sell: nothing less than West Point.

In August, Cornwallis had routed Gates at Camden, South Carolina, so West Point, anchoring the defenses of Hudson's River and southern New England, was more strategic than

ever. Gates had been sent fleeing in terror, galloping away
headlong until he was far ahead of the first waves of fugitives
from his army. He had abandoned the core of his
Continentals, who had made a last stand, bravely fighting to
the death. Gates would retire from active service, with a congressional committee established to investigate his conduct,
but that investigation would die on the vine, never pursued
by Gates's still faithful, although embarrassed, allies.

*S*O THE WAR IN THE SOUTH WAS going badly for the Americans
soon after Richard Varick joined Arnold and old friend John
Lamb, who was commandant of artillery at West Point.

Of all the posts in America at this stage of the Revolution,
West Point was perhaps the most important, for it blocked
Hudson's River to the British and was a central rebel stronghold that threatened New York City and supported operations
in northern New Jersey and New England. Varick believed
West Point had an excellent commander in Arnold, but the
poverty of the American army was evident in its lack of
ammunition. The high ramparts commanding the river and a
huge chain that blocked passage had cost millions of depreci-
ated Continental dollars, and the works should have been all
but impregnable. Before he had been there long, however,
Varick realized that West Point was not only short of ammunition, but short of soldiers: for some reason General Arnold
had been sending off detachments to outlying posts.

Despite the impressive engineering achievements that had
in three years built West Point's defenses, a powerful British
move against the fortress would encounter only a weak garri-

son desperately in need of ammunition, provisions, and equipment. These days, whatever supplies could be scraped up had to be sent to the South. It was good, therefore, that General Washington had decided to make a tour of inspection at West Point on his return trip from Hartford, where he had been conferring with the French commanders. He surely would find the means to strengthen the place, though it was well known that the American army was out of money. Washington's meeting with the French was in large part to acquire a loan or even an outright gift. As much as money, though, Washington wanted the cooperation of the French for a massive assault on New York City. As ever, he believed that only the recapture of New York would make an end to British hopes of winning the War for Independence.

Arnold's military family, including Richard Varick, knew that Washington, Knox, Lafayette, their aides, and escort were riding up the valley to spend the night at Arnold's headquarters near West Point. Samuel Shaw and James McHenry, an aide to Lafayette, had ridden on ahead to have breakfast with Arnold and his wife, Peggy, who with their infant child had just come up from Philadelphia to join her husband. For some days, Varick had been ill, and he remained in his ground-floor room of the headquarters that morning, asking to be excused from breakfast. Before Shaw and McHenry got there, Arnold entered Varick's room to ask whether certain letters had yet been answered. Varick said they had not because of his illness. A moment later, a dispatch rider appeared at the door of headquarters and handed Arnold letters from Lieutenant-colonel John Jameson, commander of dragoons patrolling south of West Point. After reading them, Arnold went upstairs to his wife's room.

Shortly thereafter, Shaw and McHenry arrived to announce that Washington's entourage was on the way, but that the general had taken a route that would allow him to inspect some redoubts on the river. Arnold showed confusion at the sight of the two aides, and called for his horse to be saddled. Telling Shaw and McHenry that he must go to West Point and would return in an hour, he rushed away. Varick, still in his room, was unable to greet Washington, who arrived a half hour later. Peggy Arnold, too, said she was too ill to come down, so the general had a hasty meal and departed for West Point.

A little later, Major David Franks, one of Arnold's longtime aides, appeared outside the window of Varick's room, seeming agitated. Something was wrong, Franks said. Arnold's barge had been seen going downriver, not up to the Point. Franks struggled with his emotions and bluntly told Varick that he believed Arnold was a villain. Franks said a spy had been captured by Jameson, and when word of it had come to Arnold, he had told the messenger to keep the news secret, then had left headquarters.

Just as Franks finished speaking, Peggy Arnold wailed from upstairs, shrieking for Varick to come to her side. He found her on the bed, appearing extremely distressed and agitated. Alexander Hamilton, who had stayed behind in the house after Washington left, also came to Mrs. Arnold, and "endeavored to soothe her by every method in my power.... It was the most affecting scene I was ever witness to."

A doctor was called. Peggy Arnold was deliriously raving, wailing about hot irons on her head, screaming that Varick had ordered her baby to be murdered. She rolled out of bed, wearing only her flimsy dressing gown, begging him on her knees to spare the child. The men tried to reassure her that her husband would soon return, but she cried out, "General Arnold will never return! He is gone! He is gone forever, there, there, there." She pointed upward. "The spirits have carried him up there! They have put hot irons in his head!"

So it went, shocking and pathetic, and frightening for these young unmarried men. They had seen so much war and bloodshed and sorrow, yet Hamilton experienced Peggy Arnold's frenzy as one of the most troubling moments of his life. Varick, too, was upset, embarrassed and disturbed to see his general's beautiful lady half-naked, her hair "disheveled and flowing about her neck," wearing too little "to be seen even by a gentleman of the family."

Washington and his staff soon returned from West Point, having startled artillery commander John Lamb, who had not been alerted that he was coming. The general was angry at the unprepared condition of the fortress. He was just as angry—and troubled—that Arnold was nowhere to be found. Then came another package from Jameson, the dragoon commander who had captured the spy. With these dispatches were not only the papers found on the spy, but a letter from the spy himself, confessing that he was none other than Major John Andre, adjutant general of the British Army. Andre had been carrying a pass signed by Benedict Arnold and had precise written descriptions of West Point's defenses and manpower—also written in Arnold's hand.

Washington was stunned. He called Hamilton and Lafayette into his room, where he declared, "Arnold has betrayed us. Whom can we trust now?"

Reports soon came in that thousands of enemy troops were on the move from New York City, sailing upriver, as if Clinton were intent on bagging Washington at West Point. Then the

wind shifted, delaying the force so that the expedition had to
be abandoned. Knowing Arnold had escaped, Washington
prepared to place John Andre on trial for his life. The "usage
of nations" of the day was to execute spies on the gibbet, just
as Nathan Hale had been executed, without military honor.

ICHARD VARICK, LIKE PEGGY ARNOLD, had been suspected
as an accomplice at first. When the truth came out, Varick
was exonerated and eventually brought onto Washington's
staff as the general's personal secretary. He became responsible for copying all official letters, many of which contained
the most intimate military secrets. In time, Mrs. Arnold and
her child were permitted to rejoin her family in Philadelphia,
while her disgraced husband joined the British Army.

Not only was Richard Varick intimately involved in the
Arnold-Andre affair, but Major Benjamin Tallmadge was the
man who had prevented Andre's being handed over to Arnold
in time for them to escape. A major in the 2nd Continental
Dragoons, and second-in-command to Jameson, Tallmadge
had objected strongly upon learning that his lieutenant-
colonel had sent the spy—then calling himself John
Anderson—to Arnold's headquarters along with the incrimi-
nating papers found secreted in the man's boot. Tallmadge
had loathed suggesting it, but he had suspected then that
Arnold and the spy were collaborating.

Hours after Jameson had dispatched Anderson to Arnold,
Tallmadge had finally convinced his commander to allow him
to fetch the man back and await the arrival of General
Washington. Tallmadge had galloped through the night in

pursuit of Anderson and his escort, and at the last moment
had prevented them from reaching Arnold. Unfortunately,
Jameson's report to Arnold about capturing Anderson could
not be stopped from getting through and alerting the traitor.

Tallmadge had remained in close confinement in a cottage
with Anderson, waiting for instructions. "I was constantly in
the room with him, and he soon became very conversable
and extremely interesting. It was very manifest that his agitation and anxiety were great." Tallmadge observed his prisoner's behavior closely, and taking note of the elegant
Anderson's "gait, especially when he turned on his heel to
retrace his course across the room." Tallmadge wrote later:
"After I saw him walk (as he did almost constantly) across the
floor, I became impressed with the belief that he had been
bred to arms."

The capture of Andre.

By three o'clock in the afternoon, the troubled Anderson asked for pen, ink, and paper, saying he wanted to write a letter to General Washington. As a gentleman of honor, he was unwilling, unable, to lie any more, and he admitted in the letter that he was none other than military secretary to Sir Henry Clinton. Tallmadge and Jameson sent the letter to Washington, who had arrived at Arnold's headquarters.

Later, as they rode together toward Washington's headquarters near West Point, Andre asked Tallmadge how he thought the general would view the situation. At first, Tallmadge had not the heart to say what was on his mind, but when Andre pressed him, he brought up the execution of Nathan Hale. Andre was startled to think his case would be considered the same as Hale's, a common spy. Tallmadge said it surely would be. He had strong cause to want revenge against the British, not only for the hanging of Hale, but also because his older brother, William, captured at Long Island, had been starved to death in a British prison. Yet, as Tallmadge spent almost every hour with Andre, before and during the trial that followed, he could not resist liking the fellow. Andre, a refined gentleman, was a talented artist, a poet and writer, and was evidently loved by many a lady, old and young, in America and Europe.

Fate had thrown them together—Tallmadge, the good-looking, Yale-educated Yankee, who by sheer ability had become one of the finest officers in the rebel army; and Andre, the refined English child of fortune, preordained by birth to command king's troops, and who likewise had become an outstanding officer.

It was a classic Revolutionary War match.

*S*IR HENRY CLINTON PLEADED FOR Andre's return, offering to trade prisoners of war for him. Washington would accept only Arnold in exchange. Although the British despised Arnold for how he had placed their beloved Andre at such risk, exchanging them was not permissible according to the dictates of military honor.

On the tribunal of fourteen generals who heard the case was Henry Knox, Andre's jovial lodging companion when they had met during Knox's mission to fetch the Ticonderoga guns in 1775. So, too, were Steuben and James Clinton. Although they all admired Andre, his composed good manners, intelligence, and courage, they could not allow personal feelings into the deliberations. Within two weeks after the capture, the verdict was reached, with sincere regrets on the part of the tribunal. Execution as a spy. They turned down Andre's only request: that he be shot rather than hanged.

Apparently that decision was not conveyed to Andre, however, for he did not know it on the day of execution as he strode past ranks of Continentals formed up at attention, surrounded by thousands of spectators, civilians and soldiers, watching in profound silence.

Tallmadge later wrote: "As I was with him most of the time from his capture, and walked with him as he went to the place of execution, I never discovered any emotions of fear.... When he came in sight of the gibbet, he appeared to be startled, and inquired with some emotion whether he was not to be shot."

"How hard is my fate!" Andre said softly, when he heard he would die at the end of a rope. "But it will soon be over."

With that, Tallmadge said later, "I then shook hands with him under the gallows and retired."

He did not see Andre, the man he had captured, climb onto the wagon beneath the gibbet and stand calmly on his own coffin, then place the noose snugly around his own neck, and blindfold himself. Even after the instant of death, silence hung over the masses who had witnessed it. It seemed none of them had wanted John Andre to die. Nor did General Washington, who sat most of that day at a table in his headquarters, trying to work on official business.

*B*ENEDICT ARNOLD BECAME A BRITISH BRIGADIER GENERAL and served in the Virginia campaigns, where Greene, Lafayette, and Steuben soon went to perform with skill and stubborn determination, losing battles to the tenacious Cornwallis, but ultimately winning the South. John Laurens would be exchanged and join these three, again to be caught up in the fierce fighting, including in his home state of South Carolina.

In October 1780, his father, Henry Laurens, was captured aboard ship while sailing to the Netherlands to negotiate a loan and treaty. He was thrown into the Tower of London, where doomed political prisoners could expect to live out the rest of their lives, if not executed first. The Tower would be Washington's fate, too, if the Revolution were defeated.

In November of that year, Benjamin Tallmadge led a daring raid across Long Island Sound, destroying enemy provisions and taking prisoners. He would become Washington's most active spy master for the rest of the war, working with secret agents in Long Island and New York City.

VICTORY

*T*HE YEAR 1781 WAS A MEMORY ALL ITS OWN. It began with mutiny in the Pennsylvania Continental regiments stationed in New Jersey. A Pennsylvania officer was killed when he tried to stop them from defying authority. Though free-flowing rum after New Year's had contributed its part, the men had plenty of reason to be in a fury—they were unpaid, poorly clothed, hungry, and what few Continental dollars they had were just worthless paper. Meanwhile new recruits were being paid large bounties by the states to join up. The mutineers were loyal, war-weary veterans who believed Congress cared nothing about them.

Winter was the worst time of all for the troops, but as understandable as their anger might be, no army—no matter how much it suffered—could survive if mutiny was not put down unhesitatingly. No commanding general could countenance mutiny and still maintain discipline, still keep his army in the field. These mutineers were marching to Philadelphia and Congress, bringing their cannon along. Writing from his headquarters at New Windsor, on Hudson's River, Washington warned Congress not to flee, or matters would worsen. The city might even be sacked, and other troops likely would join in until mutiny blazed throughout the army, beyond the point of reconciliation. The British were waiting for just such an opportunity. Already, their agents were talking to the troops, trying to foment insurrection, promising royal pardons and cash payments. Washington called his staff together, prepared to ride to the point of trouble—until he learned that the troops in his own encampment were restless, that they, too, might rise up. He dared not leave them.

At length, the Pennsylvania mutineers sobered up, cooled down, and stopped at Princeton. There, they and their officers negotiated terms that were costly to the army: one-half were allowed to be discharged on the spot, the rest given furloughs until springtime, and financial promises were made. For the time being, the Pennsylvania line existed only on paper. And the troubles were not over. Soon afterward, two hundred New Jersey Continentals rose up and made demands similar to those of the Pennsylvanians. There could be no such negotiation now. An example had to be made, harsh though it would be. The entire war effort depended on the army's remaining disciplined and on duty.

"The existence of the army called for an example," the general said. Soldiers could not "dictate terms to their country." It did not matter that the New Jersey mutineers soon negotiated with their officers and went back to their huts. It was too late. They found themselves surrounded by other troops, ordered out of their huts and paraded without their arms. Three ringleaders were arrested, immediately tried, two pardoned, and one shot by a weeping firing squad.

*T*HE ARMY WAS REORGANIZED THAT YEAR with many regiments consolidated. Connecticut took the unusual step of placing all its Negro soldiers in one company a hundred and fifty strong. David Humphreys, who used his influence to establish the unit—the first of its kind—was nominally its commander. Humphreys is said to have been one of the first whites to recognize the black soldier's qualities. According to the rolls, more than seven hundred and fifty blacks, in fourteen regiments, had served in Washington's army in 1778.

Early in 1781, welcome reports came in that Daniel Morgan had won a critical battle over the loyalists at Cowpens, South Carolina. Soon after, in a close contest at Guilford Courthouse, North Carolina, Cornwallis forced Greene to withdraw, although the Americans retreated in good order. Then the armies of these two excellent field generals began a deadly dance, with Cornwallis always in pursuit, Greene striking back when he could; but the British had no replacements for an army operating deep inland, and Cornwallis grew weaker with every clash.

In this time, Alexander Hamilton's restless ambition brought him into conflict with Washington. Hamilton was sick of never-ending paperwork, sick of being scolded when Washington was in an ill humor, and sick of being at the general's beck and call every moment, day and night. He asked for a field command, but Washington wanted him at headquarters. Then Hamilton was deeply disappointed not to be given the mission undertaken by his friend, John Laurens. Washington sent Laurens to France to convey the crucial need for immediate financial, as well as military, support. Without both, Washington said, the army would be capable of no more than a "feeble and expiring effort the next campaign.... We are at the end of our tether."

Unrelieved stress on everyone flared up one day in April, with a petty argument between the general and Hamilton. Washington complained about the aide's failure to promptly respond to his call, and Hamilton resigned on the spot. Washington was willing to let it go and start again, but Hamilton was through with the headquarters staff. Losing him was painful for Washington, who greatly admired Hamilton: "There are few men to be found of his age who have a more general knowledge than he possesses, and none whose soul is more firmly engaged in the cause, or who exceeds him in probity and sterling value."

Humphreys and Varick stepped into the breach, Varick to plant himself in an office near Poughkeepsie, New York, where he would laboriously copy all official letters into a bound book, and Humphreys to serve as Washington's right hand at headquarters.

A few weeks after Hamilton's resignation, word came from Laurens in Paris that the French were ordering another major fleet to America, and King Louis's court had promised a fortune in cash to support the rebellion. This was exactly what Washington had been waiting for. With the French navy operating in and around New York Bay, the Franco-American army could attack the city and end the war. The French had other ideas, however. They wanted to send their naval forces into the Chesapeake Bay, attack British shipping there, and strike at smaller enemy-held ports.

That July, the main French army of five thousand men under Comte de Rochambeau joined Washington's force of roughly the same size. They combined their operations in southern New York State, anticipating the next offensive. Officially, Rochambeau was second-in-command to Washington, but of course the Virginian's plans had to be acceptable to the Frenchman. By now, the French held a high opinion of Washington, both as a strategist and as a leader who had kept an embattled little army in the field against all odds.

The French arrived with much pomp, in their magnificent uniforms and with dazzling accouterments and equipment; they were pleasantly surprised to see the impoverished Americans so well-disciplined and healthy. It was especially impressive that the American officers rode such excellent horses. The Continentals might be shoddily uniformed, but they were obviously fine soldiers. Washington was pleased to hear praise from the French, one of whom "tremendously admired" the American troops, saying, "It is incredible that soldiers composed of men of every age, even of children of fifteen, of whites and blacks, almost naked, unpaid, and rather poorly fed, can march so well and withstand fire so steadfastly." Another remarked that the Americans were "intended for action, not for show." One embarrassment Washington and his officers suffered from was their inability at joint staff meetings to provide tables in keeping with what the French were used to. The French officers did not complain in public, although one grumbled that the Americans made weak coffee.

A Frenchman—used to high-ranking officers affecting exaggerated poses whenever they reviewed columns of troops—observed Washington, lost in thought and staring intently, as his men went marching by. It was remarkable, and admirable, that the American commander did not posture or exhibit the slight-

A teacher and intellectual from Connecticut, David Humphreys served as a staff officer throughout the war, joining Washington's headquarters staff in 1780 and becoming a key aide who remained with Washington after the war.

est expression of self-importance. Perhaps Washington's thoughts were busy with plans for attacking New York. By now, there was mutual respect between his army and the French, promising great things when the campaign got underway.

$\int$ IR HENRY CLINTON IN NEW YORK had plenty to worry about, and all Franco-American probing raids were alertly countered. Meantime, in the South, Cornwallis found himself pursuing Lafayette and Steuben, too, and their little army was even harder to catch than Greene's. The Americans concentrated on striking at smaller British detachments, doing so effectively. Southern militias were rising against Cornwallis as his campaign moved into Virginia. Though he won small victories, his aggressiveness put him in danger of running out of men. He needed a base on the coast, where the Royal Navy could resupply him and bring reinforcements, so he made his way to Yorktown.

By August, when Rochambeau reported that a French fleet loaded with soldiers and marines was due to arrive somewhere on the southern coast in a few weeks, Washington conceded that there was another campaign to be fought. Instead of the one he had envisioned against Clinton and New York City, this campaign would mass all the force at his disposal against the unsuspecting Cornwallis and his army. It would require a forced march of almost four hundred miles from the allies' positions facing New York City, and it depended on the French fleet's arriving at just the right time to prevent Cornwallis's escape or reinforcement by sea.

Washington went into action. He sent for his best troops and commanders, had Knox bring the artillery together, called Van Cortlandt down from upstate with veteran Yorkers, and alerted Lafayette and Steuben to prepare to cut off Cornwallis's retreat overland. John Laurens managed to return from France just in time to join the expedition.

Washington had to surprise and overwhelm Cornwallis, arguably the ablest of all the British generals in America. The army would include George and James Clinton, Steuben, Lafayette, Lamb, Tallmadge, Hull, Shaw, Walker, Humphreys, Jackson, and Hamilton, too—Washington gave him command of an elite light infantry battalion, with Hamilton's friend, Nicholas Fish, as second. McDougall had given up active duty and was a delegate for New York to the Continental Congress—a good place for an ally of

Washington's to be. The movement of the Franco-American armies toward Virginia would have to be kept secret for as long as possible, and for several weeks the ultimate object of their marches would not be made clear even to high-ranking officers.

The French fleet with its reinforcements must arrive in the Chesapeake before the British Navy appeared there to block its entry, and Sir Henry Clinton must be tricked into thinking Washington's movements across New Jersey in concert with the French army were maneuvers preparatory to attacking strongly defended Staten Island. Washington ordered encampments built in New Jersey, as if to house his army, complete with supply depots and bake ovens. To blunt enemy reconnaissance, strong skirmishing parties drove in Clinton's scouts and pickets around the New York defensive perimeter. Washington's and Rochambeau's main forces moved southward in gradual stages, until they finally made a dash for Philadelphia.

Now committed to the Yorktown campaign, the American and French armies marched as fast as possible through terrible summer heat, crossing the Delaware River before the British realized what was happening. By then it was too late for Clinton to attempt to divert them by a sally in strength from New York. Everything unfolded according to plan, and when the French fleet miraculously appeared at the mouth of the Chesapeake, driving away British ships and landing thousands more troops to join Washington and Rochambeau, Cornwallis found himself pinned against the water's edge. Time, however, did not favor the Franco-American allies, for the British Navy was still powerful and might strike at the outnumbered French fleet. French ships, with few safe harbors close by, were also vulnerable to the storms sweeping up

The older of the two Clinton brothers in a prominent family that came from near Newburgh, New York, James Clinton had served in the French and Indian War; in the Revolution, he participated in the first invasion of Canada, took part in the defense of the Hudson River, participated in the 1779 expedition against the Iroquois, and won distinction for valor at Yorktown.

the coast this time of year. Cornwallis had to be defeated after as short a siege as possible.

That meant heavy artillery bombardments must devastate the British positions and destroy the enemy's will to resist; daring frontal attacks must be launched against key redoubts protecting Cornwallis's front lines. It also meant Washington had to inspire his troops by finding them a month's pay in hard money, which Congress could not provide. Rochambeau dug into his war chest, giving a third of it to Washington, raising the spirits of the troops who were on the way to lay siege to Yorktown.

As the allies set about squeezing Cornwallis, Washington took the opportunity to visit Mount Vernon for the first time since the outbreak of war in 1775. Martha was there, awaiting him and his headquarters staff. In a day or so the French general staff arrived in all their glory, and the next phase of this momentous campaign was planned at Mount Vernon. In his gracious mansion overlooking the broad Potomac, surrounded by glittering French officers, Washington could savor a heady moment of power and promise such as he had never experienced before. He also could take pride in his own accomplished staff of officers, which mingled easily with their elegant allies. Present, too, were his three little step-grandchildren and their parents, Martha's son, Jacky Custis, and his wife, Nelly.

In his mid-twenties, Jacky was an irresponsible young man, pampered by his mother, and had never shown interest in joining the army. In fact, he was somewhat intimidated by his stepfather, so it was a complete surprise to Washington when Jacky asked to be a volunteer aide on his staff. Knowing the imminent dangers, the need for physical endurance, and his stepson's tendency to self-indulgence, Washington was reluctant at first, but Martha wanted it, and he agreed.

*O*CTOBER 9 WAS CLEAR AND PLEASANT AS WASHINGTON stood on the allied earthworks, facing Yorktown across the sandy plains, the blue sea horizon on his right. A loaded French siege cannon awaited the lighted linstock in the general's hand. It was precisely three in the afternoon. The Continental standard was run up over the American batteries, the white flag of France hoisted over theirs. That was the signal to begin. Washington held the linstock to the touchhole, and the gun roared, jerking back as it sent its projectile toward

Cornwallis's army. The ball could be heard striking from house to house as it passed through the town.

The entire British artillery erupted in response to Washington's shot, which had killed or injured several British officers seated at their dinner table. French and American guns in turn opened fire at the British fortifications and at shipping in the York River.

The savage bombardment of Yorktown would continue for more than a week. From the start, the enemy's artillery was overwhelmed by the more numerous, more powerful French and American guns. The cannonade went on relentlessly. At night the sky was streaked with fiery mortar shells soaring up and falling into the town, or upon the anchored ships and setting them ablaze. Shells from the British and the allies crisscrossed the sky, like meteors, whistling down to land with a thud, soon to explode.

Although at first many of the American shells had been duds and failed to go off, before long the accuracy and effectiveness of the rebel guns had begun winning the praise of the French. Washington's artillery was handled by Knox, Lamb, and Shaw, and also by young lieutenant Robert Burnett, a New Yorker. Burnett had been only thirteen years of age when the war started, although he had temporarily helped guard German prisoners in 1777, when they passed through his neighborhood near New Windsor.

One by one, the British guns were knocked from their mountings, their crews wiped out. The enemy cannon fire was diminished with each passing day, and Yorktown became a hell on earth for the seven thousand soldiers and the hundreds of civilians trapped there. Cornwallis faced sixteen thousand men in the Franco-American armies. Yet for all the destruction wreaked by the allies' guns, artillery alone would not bring surrender quickly enough. French and American engineers steadily extended the siege works, with trenches dug after dark, moving ever closer to the British positions, bringing guns to bear at favorable angles, and offering staging areas from which infantry attacks could be launched.

On the night of October 14, Washington stood on the grand battery with generals Henry Knox and Benjamin Lincoln and their staffs, everyone peering into the dark, listening for the start of attacks against two forward redoubts. The French would assault one, and the American elite light infantry, including Hamilton, Fish, and Laurens, would attack the other. Hamilton had been chosen by Washington to lead the vanguard of his assault. Bayonets were fixed, and muskets were kept unloaded so that no accidental firing would alert the enemy. It was work for the bayonet tonight, as it had been at Stony Point. At any moment, Hamilton and his men would rush through the darkness into the deep ditch below the redoubt walls, clamber over pointed stakes protruding from the ground, and fight their way through a tangle of sharp branches and small trees barricading the top of the earthworks.

Suddenly, the generals heard British muskets firing, men shouting and crying out in anger and pain. It went on for less than ten minutes, and then fell quiet. The redoubt was taken. The French captured theirs shortly afterward.

"It is done," Washington said then, turning to Knox. "And well done." With that, he called for his horse.

After this night, further resistance by Cornwallis was useless. At ten in the morning on October 17, the anniversary of Burgoyne's surrender at Saratoga, a lone drummer boy appeared on the British parapet and beat out a signal the Americans did not at first recognize. Then a redcoat officer appeared, waving a white handkerchief. The drummer was beating a request for a parley. Lord Cornwallis wanted a twenty-four-hour truce to negotiate terms of surrender. The allied guns fell silent.

For the American army, this was the most shining moment of the Revolution. Washington was in his glory, although it was a pity his stepson was not there to witness the surrender, for Jacky had fallen ill with fever and was sent to a friend's home to recover.

ON MID-AFTERNOON OF OCTOBER 19, A warm day for autumn, General Washington sat on a big bay horse, awaiting the approach of Brigadier-general Charles O'Hara, Cornwallis's second-in-command. Cornwallis had said he was too ill to attend the surrender ceremony. The Comte de Rochambeau was on horseback in front of his own troops, who were paraded facing Washington and his army.

The British officers appeared, riding slowly between the ranks of the victors—the Americans on one side, in faded blues, buff, homespun, and drab, and, on the other, the French in their splendid whites. At the last moment, O'Hara turned his horse toward Rochambeau, intending to surrender his sword to him instead of Washington, but a mounted French officer headed him off. Rochambeau gestured toward the Virginian, and O'Hara had no choice but to present his sword to George Washington.

The surrender at Yorktown, with Washington directing O'Hara to Lincoln.

Instead of accepting the sword, Washington indicated General Benjamin Lincoln, his own second-in-command, to whom the sword was finally presented in formal surrender.

Afterward, the defeated British army marched out of its works, with drums beating unrhythmically, as if the drummers did not care how they sounded. Their musicians played slow and solemn tunes as the troops marched to a field to lay down their arms. As inglorious as the defeat was for the British, so were the honors plentiful for Washington's officers. Philip van Cortlandt, James Clinton, Hamilton, Fish, and Laurens (who was on the commission that negotiated the surrender terms) were specifically merited for valor under fire, and Knox and his artillery for their effectiveness. Baron von Steuben personally planted an American flag on the British works, and James Clinton's brigade had the honor of receiving the captured flags. Washington did David Humphreys the exquisite compliment of ordering him to carry those flags to Philadelphia, to be laid at the feet of the amazed and delighted Continental Congress.

Washington wrote a brief report of the victory and sent it to Congress, scarcely mentioning himself: "I have the Honor to inform Congress, that a Reduction of the British Army under the Command of Lord Cornwallis, is most happily effected. The unremitting Ardor which actuated every Officer and Soldier in the combined Army in this Occasion, has principally led to this Important Event, at an earlier period than my most sanguine Hope had induced me to expect."

Once this dispatch was on its way, Washington rode homeward to enjoy the momentous occasion with his family, well aware that his greatest triumph had virtually assured victory in the Revolution. Before he could go home, however, he learned that Jacky Custis was gravely ill and being cared for in a friend's house. Washington hurried there, and just as he entered the room where Jacky lay abed, his stepson died.

Colonel David Humphreys carries captured flags from Yorktown to the Continental Congress in Philadelphia; entitled "Delivery of the Standards," this painting is thought to have been executed by a Danish artist when Humphreys was in Europe between 1784-86, as a secretary to Thomas Jefferson.

The Long

Farewell

*T*HE REVOLUTION DRAGGED ON FOR TWO more years as peace terms were discussed and rediscussed in Paris. In all that time, Washington had to keep an army in existence, or the British might at any moment change course and resume the war. His greatest fear was that American complacency—especially in Congress and the state capitals—would be so pervasive that, once the French departed, the British would pounce on the first opportunity to strike from New York.

The French troops were stationed in the South most of this time, coming north in 1782-83 to winter close to the American headquarters at New Windsor, near Newburgh, New York. Washington's headquarters were alternately at New Windsor or at Rocky Hill, near Princeton. Sir Henry Clinton resigned, the third British commander to do so, and was replaced by Sir Guy Carleton, who came to New York from Canada. Although Carleton was much respected by the Americans as a man who preferred peace to war, the army remained prepared—except when young blades such as Fish and Lafayette were out sledding down the New Windsor hillsides with local girls.

Early in 1782, Henry Laurens was released from the Tower after much agitation by influential Britishers who were disgusted by their government's bringing on the war to begin with. Laurens went to Paris to help negotiate the peace treaty. Horatio Gates came out of retirement, to be given his rank as second-in-command to Washington. Gates would be kept busy with garrison duty and overseeing positions on Hudson's River.

In May 1782, Washington was shocked to receive a seven-page letter from Colonel Lewis Nicola, commander of the invalid corps, saying that the general who had won victory through seemingly insurmountable difficulties ought to be the one to lead it in the coming peace. Nicola plainly stated that Washington should be America's first king. The general was profoundly troubled by the letter, especially when he learned that other officers felt the same, and were willing to stand by him if he wanted to assume the crown. Among these officers was the impressionable Robert Burnett.

The general drafted a harsh reply, which he asked his aides to read and sign as witnesses that he rejected out of hand the very thought of being made an American king. To Nicola, he wrote: "Be assured, sir, no occurrence in the course of the war has given me more painful sensations than your information of there being such ideas existing in the army as you have expressed it and I must view with abhorrence and reprehend with severity." Washington asked in his reply what he had done to have encouraged Nicola to send such a letter "which to me seems big with the greatest mischiefs that can befall my country. If I am not deceived in the knowledge of myself, you could not have found a person to whom your schemes are more disagreeable."

*T*HE NORTHERN THEATER REMAINED QUIET, although skirmishing and raiding continued in the South, where the American commander, Nathanael Greene, controlled all but the enemy-occupied cities of Savannah and Charleston. In one of those inconsequential clashes near Charleston in August of 1782, the rash John Laurens was killed. The blow to Washington was a hard one.

More than ever, the general was weary of the service, worried that the peace terms would not be settled unless the Americans took to the field again, as he wrote to a friend:

> I pant for retirement, and am persuaded that an end of our warfare is not to be obtained but by vigorous exertions.... I can truly say that the first wish of my Soul is to return speedily into the bosom of that country, which gave me birth, and, in the sweet enjoyment of my domestic happiness and the company of a few friends, to end my days in quiet, when I shall be called from this stage.

That August, in part to boost morale, Washington decreed that privates and noncommissioned officers would be eligible for a "Badge of Military Merit" in reward of unusual gallantry and for "extraordinary fidelity and essential services." To be worn on the left breast, the badge would be "the figure of a heart in purple cloth or silk." Nicholas Fish was one of the officers on the first panel selected to decide which candidates deserved the Purple Heart. Only three would be awarded before the war was over, all to men from Connecticut, two of whom had served in operations behind enemy lines at the direction of Benjamin Tallmadge.

About the Purple Heart, Washington said: "The road to glory in a patriot army and a free country is thus opened to all."

*T*HE PEACE WAS PROVISIONALLY SIGNED in November 1782, but the final document had to be officially approved, and the occupying British forces would not depart until then. Washington was determined not to leave the army until everything was settled and the redcoats left New York. He felt himself aging, in part because of trouble with his teeth and his eyes. He ordered new false teeth, and purchased a set of reading glasses, a rarity in America.

Meanwhile, unrest flared anew in the American army, which still suffered from Congress's negligence and lack of pay. Massachusetts regiments began to agitate, demanding that their home state take care of them. A committee of officers headed by Alexander McDougall presented itself to Congress in Philadelphia in the name of the officer corps, to resolve the issue of back pay and pensions. Congress, as usual, referred them to a committee.

In February 1783, Washington reflected upon what had been achieved, and he wrote to Greene, who since early in the war had shared the burdens of the highest level of command:

> If historiographers should be hardy enough to fill the page of history with the advantages that have been gained with unequal numbers (on the part of America) in the course of this contest, and attempt to relate the distressing circumstances under which they have been obtained, it is more than probable that posterity will bestow on their labors the epithet of fiction.

To save money, Congress resolved to further consolidate regiments, thus reducing the need for officers. Men would summarily be thrown out of the army, to be sent home destitute, with nothing more than a vague promise that they would be paid sometime in the future. Among the officers, this bred even more bitterness against Congress, and although no one still suggested Washington crown himself, the consensus of many was that he should lead them to Philadelphia in a threat to Congress. Some were willing to go so far as to undertake a coup if not treated fairly. Just the threat of force would be enough to cow Congress, so ran the line of thinking; having Washington at their head would be enough to demonstrate their virtue, that they were not trying to overthrow the republic they had fought to establish. The officers' love for Washington, the budding conspirators believed, would keep them all in line and united.

Washington knew enough of the low morale of the army that he chose to winter with it at his cramped and drafty quarters at New Windsor, overlooking Hudson's River. At first, word of the anti-Congress conspiracy did not reach the commander-in-chief's ears, for the agitators wanted their plot more fully developed before the general could interfere. Even Hamilton, now a congressional delegate from New York, saw an opportunity in the army's unrest and was in favor of making a military move to shake up Congress once and for all. He wanted to force Congress and the states to act decisively and create a strong central government, a federal organization with the power to tax in order to pay its way. Hamilton believed a rising of the officers would compel Congress to take the necessary action to pay them, and it ultimately would be for the good of the United American States. He even led

Congress to believe that the army would not lay down its arms until all its grievances were addressed satisfactorily.

One member of McDougall's committee representing the officers to Congress concurred, saying, "the temper of the army was such that they did not reason or deliberate coolly on consequences, and therefore a disappointment might throw them blindly into extremities."

The Revolution was approaching a precipice from which it might not be able to turn. The result could be civil war and possibly a dictatorship. One prominent politician of the day wrote to another, "The army have swords in their hands. You know enough of the history of mankind to know much more than I have said and possibly much more than they themselves think of."

Then Washington heard from Hamilton that supplies and back pay were unlikely to be forthcoming very soon, and that Hamilton believed the officers were reluctant to lay down their arms without "obtaining justice" from Congress. Hamilton gave his former mentor some serious advice: if the officers resolved to make a demonstration against Congress, "the difficulty will be to keep a complaining and suffering army within the bounds of moderation. This your Excellency's influence must effect."

In other words, Hamilton was advising Washington to confront Congress at the head of his army— "in case of extremity, to guide the torrent and bring order." Otherwise, the officers might mutiny without him. Another letter from a member of Congress said, "Reports are freely circulated here that there are dangerous combinations in the army, and within a few days past it has been said, they are about to declare they will not disband until their demands are complied with."

These "sinister" combinations were out to damage Washington's reputation, the friend said.

Washington soon discovered that some of his old critics in the army were at the root of the conspiracy, and among them was Gates—silent and deceitful as ever, but as second-in-command, he would be the man to lead an action against Congress if Washington did not.

*I*T ALL CAME TO A HEAD IN MARCH OF 1783, when Washington learned of an anonymous letter circulating through the army that was stationed in and around the cantonment at New Windsor. The letter called for a mass meeting of the officers the next day in order to consider how to have Congress redress their grievances, which McDougall's committee had apparently failed to do.

The author wrote that he had, "till lately—very lately—believed in the justice of his country," but "Faith has its limits, as well as temper." Did the reader, he asked, believe his country would welcome him home from the war "with tears of gratitude and smiles of admiration," or "is it rather a country that tramples upon your rights, disdains your cries, and insults your distresses?…"

Washington bridled, seeing mutiny raise its head in an unauthorized meeting of officers. The first thing he did was to assert his authority and tell the army that he objected to "such disorderly proceedings." Instead, he called a meeting of his own, to be held a few days later, on March 15. Although he implied he would not attend, he did require that the meeting

Commander of the rear-guard at Washington's entry into New York City, Robert Burnett was from near Newburgh, New York, and was thought to be one of the officers who for a time believed Washington should become king.

be in the charge of the ranking officer present, who then would report the proceedings to Washington. That officer would be Horatio Gates, a willing tool of the conspirators.

Before the meeting, a second anonymous letter circulated, approving the change of date, and suggesting that Washington might very well condone what they were doing.

*T*HE TEMPLE WAS A LARGE HALL, built by the army for religious services, festivities, and gatherings, and on the day of the meeting it held hundreds of officers sitting on benches, winter capes thrown across their legs, boots and shoes dirty with icy mud. Gates and several other officers were at a table on the dais. The mood was a mingling of anger and hurt feelings, the conversation surly and buzzing loudly as Gates prepared to get underway.

Then a door off the dais opened, and through it came General Washington. Startled, the hundreds sprang to their feet, at attention, a sudden silence coming over them. Washington was visibly agitated. Gates had no choice but to ask that the general address the officers, who then were told to take their seats. Washington stood before them, looking over all those faces of men who had endured so much for the country. For him.

First, he apologized for appearing at the meeting, saying it had by no means been his intention when first he called for them to assemble today. Now, however, he believed it essential that he give his sentiments to the army regarding the anonymous letters, and so he had committed his thoughts to writing. He drew out what he had written, and began with a direct rebuke typical of his disarming style, a rebuke that set the tone for his address:

> Gentlemen. By an anonymous summons an attempt has been made to convene you together. How inconsistent with the rules of propriety, how unmilitary, and how subversive of all good order and discipline—let the good sense of the army decide.

He complimented the anonymous author as being "entitled to much credit for the goodness of his pen, and I could wish he had as much credit for the rectitude of his heart." The officers were troubled to hear their beloved general say the original meeting had been called by an author who insinuated "the darkest suspicion, to effect the blackest designs." If most of them had no real grasp of the "insidious purposes" of the anonymous letters, Washington set them straight. They were, he said,

> calculated to impress the mind with an idea of pre-meditated injustice in all the sovereign power of the United States, and rouse all those resentments which must unavoidably flow from such a belief; that the secret mover of this scheme, whoever he may be, intended to take advantage of the passions, while they were warmed by the recollection of past distresses, without giving them time for cool, deliberate thinking, and that composure of mind which is so necessary to give dignity and stability to measures....

The listeners were enthralled, flushing with embarrassment to hear that Washington opposed the calling of an "irregular and hasty meeting," but that he wanted to give them

> every opportunity, consistent with your own honor and the dignity of the army, to make known your grievances. If my conduct heretofore has not evinced to you, that I have been a faithful friend to the army, my declaration of it at this time would be equally unavailing and improper.

What soldier could doubt Washington's feelings for the army? The officers were chastened to think that he, in turn, might doubt their regard for him. He went on, and it was excruciating to hear him say, "I have never left your side one moment," to hear him tell how his "heart has ever expanded with joy" when he heard praise for the army. But, as for the anonymous author who had called upon the officers never to sheathe their swords until they "have obtained full and ample justice,"

> Can he be a friend to his country? Rather is he not an insidious foe? Some emissary, perhaps from New York, plotting…ruin…by sowing the seeds of discord and separation between the civil and military powers of the continent?

Most of the men in the room well knew that the author of the anonymous letters was Major John Armstrong, an aide to Horatio Gates. An "emissary" from New York, of course, meant an agent of the British, who still occupied the city.

And so the address went, and the hearts of the officers melted like the winter puddles around their feet. The general called for "a moment's reflection," to permit exercise of their best judgment, in which he had such faith. He went so far as to assure them that he believed Congress would succeed in finding the funds to pay them. He made a promise "in this public and solemn manner" that he would never rest until the army had received full justice at the hands of Congress, and he asked them to reject the anonymous letters, and to offer their country

> one more distinguished proof of unexampled patriotism and patient virtue…and you will, by the dignity of your conduct, afford occasion for posterity to

say... "Had this day been wanting, the world had never seen the last stage of perfection, to which human nature is capable of attaining."

The men were swept with emotion and inspiration.

Washington closed by offering to read a letter from a member of Congress who told of the latest measures taken to answer the needs of the army. The uneasy audience stirred in their seats, glancing around at one another, hoping the general could, indeed, assure that Congress would take definite steps to secure their pay and pensions. Washington fumbled with the letter, squinting at it, starting to read hesitantly, and then he stopped. Reaching into his pocket, he drew out the spectacles.

Seated in the audience, Samuel Shaw was as mesmerized as the rest when the commander-in-chief put on his glasses and begged the indulgence of the officers, "observing at the same time, that he had grown gray in their service, and now found himself going blind. There was something so natural, so unaffected, in this appeal, as rendered it superior to the most studied oratory; it forced its way to the heart, and you might see sensibility moisten every eye."

Thus did Washington turn aside the conspiracy that could have stirred up mutiny in the disappointed, yet patriotic, officers.

A MONTH LATER, ON APRIL 19, the anniversary of the battles of Lexington and Concord, the army celebrated the announcement of final peace terms. The war was over. The British would withdraw in a few months, evacuating New York and taking thousands of displaced loyalists with them. All that was left now was for the politicians on both sides to sign the "definitive treaty."

To maintain relations among the Revolutionary officers, Knox, Steuben, and Shaw laid the groundwork for a fraternity called the Society of the Cincinnati, and Washington agreed to be its first president. Cincinnatus was a Roman hero who fought for his people, and after the war returned to the plow, giving up the privileges of power.

That spring, the first Purple Heart was awarded to Sergeant Elijah Churchill of East Windsor, Connecticut, the chief noncommissioned officer who had joined Benjamin Tallmadge on a whaleboat raid across Long Island Sound in 1780. Seeing one of their own thus recognized gave a lift to the morale of average soldiers. But then the entire army was dismayed when Congress—confident that peace had finally been achieved—ordered the regiments disbanded piecemeal. The men would be sent home, ostensibly on furloughs, but obviously being discharged without the pay due them, other than promissory notes that were not backed up by hard money.

Washington remonstrated with Congress, but at the same time he realized that once the disbanding procedure began it would be best to get it over with quickly and the troops dispersed before armed mutiny again threatened. In fact, some recently enlisted Pennsylvania troops marched on

Philadelphia, but they were persuaded by cooler heads to be patient and just go home.

Then Congress simply adjourned, leaving all the army's financial affairs unresolved. Officers and men went home embarrassed, some without a penny of hard cash in their pockets. The officers in particular were deeply disappointed in Washington for promising to see to their needs when he had spoken to them in the Temple at New Windsor. It was apparent he had failed to make any headway with Congress regarding their pay or guarantees of future compensation, land grants, or pensions.

In August, a frustrated, weary Washington wrote to a friend in New York:

> I only wait (and with anxious impatience) the arrival of the definitive treaty, that I may take leave of my Military Employments and by bidding adieu to Public life, forever enjoy in the shades of retirement that ease and tranquillity to which, for more than eight years, I have been an entire stranger, and for which, a mind which has been constantly on the stretch during that period, and perplexed with a thousand embarrassing circumstances, often times without a ray of light to guide it, stands much in need.

That autumn, Washington wrote a farewell to the army, but there was little army left to read it to. As for the remaining officers, they expressed their disappointment by sending Washington a coldly worded letter of thanks for his service. A farewell banquet had been planned with the officers and the

General George Washington bids farewell to his officers in the Long Room of Fraunces Tavern in New York, on December 4, 1783.

general, but at the last moment the unhappy officers canceled it and left the army.

To Congress, Washington wrote sadly, "The sensibility occasioned by a parting scene under such peculiar circumstances, will not admit of description." He would work for their welfare in years to come, but now it seemed the men of the army had been callously betrayed by an ungrateful country.

Most ranking officers, including Greene, Lafayette, and Lincoln, had returned home. Those officers who answered Washington's last-minute invitation to Fraunces Tavern on December 4, 1783, were men who did not want to part with him without expressing their feelings of love and admiration. Among them, perhaps in part to increase the number of men in the room, were several of John Lamb's junior artillery officers, as well as the youthful Robert Burnett, who had commanded the rear guard that marched into the city a few days ago.

The officers had not been in the Fraunces Tavern Long Room more than a few minutes, most chatting, partaking of food and drink, others reflecting on the past, when—

*T*HERE WAS A STIRRING, AND EVERYONE rose. His Excellency was there, standing in the doorway, impeccable in his dark blue coat, gold epaulets, buff waistcoat and breeches, boots gleaming, sword at his side.

A hush came over the room.

His Excellency strode across the floor toward the banquet table. Men moved aside, some bowing, hats held to the chest. He sampled the food with a hand that trembled slightly. There was a breathless silence. He filled a glass, then turned to face them. Raising his wine, prepared to toast, he paused for the hurried, clumsy rush as empty glasses were refilled.

Then he looked around the room.

"With a heart full of love and gratitude, I now take leave of you."

Hearts were bursting.

"I most devoutly wish that your latter days may be as prosperous and happy as your former ones have been glorious and honorable."

Murmured assent. They all drank.

His eyes were suffused with tears, though his voice was steady: "I cannot come to each of you, but shall feel obliged if each of you will come and take me by the hand."

Knox, the new commander-in-chief, was first to turn to him, awkwardly moving to grasp his hand. They embraced, incapable of speaking, and he kissed Knox's cheek. Blinded by tears, Knox turned away. Hamilton came next. Neither man spoke as they embraced.

So it was with all of them. In heart-rending expressions of their love, each officer gripped his hand, and he embraced them. No words, only sighs, sobs, and weeping.

When every man had said goodbye, His Excellency went toward the door. It was unbearable to think they would not see him again. At the door, he turned, and raised a hand to his officers one last time.

It was done. And well done.

THE END

After the farewell, Washington takes a boat across the Hudson River to New Jersey to begin the journey to Annapolis, Maryland, where Congress awaits his resignation as commander-in-chief.

END NOTES

*T*HERE ARE FEW EXTANT eyewitness reports about the flag the redcoats left behind on Fort George and how it was replaced with the Stars and Stripes. The existing stories vary, and the version told here is largely based on James Riker's 1883 pamphlet, "Evacuation Day, 1783." The author viewed the New York State Library's copy, which is the very one Riker signed and gave as a gift to historian Benson Lossing. It makes sense that rather than nailing the American flag to the pole, as some histories claim, Van Arsdale climbed up and refitted a halyard to raise it in the usual way.

Evidence that Washington stayed in Fraunces Tavern during the re-occupation of New York City is found in *George Washington's Accounts of Expenses While Commander-in-chief of the Continental Army*. In his role as commander-in-chief, Washington asked for no other compensation than that his expenses be paid, and, as he did throughout his life, he kept meticulous financial records. The Library of Congress has placed on-line the original documents, with the annotations of Washington historian John C. Fitzpatrick. This collection has Washington's bill to Samuel Fraunces for the period November 25 through December 4.

Fitzpatrick believed that Washington stayed at Fraunces Tavern, and staff at both the Library of Congress and the University of Virginia concur that the evidence clearly validates that conclusion. The expense record has no other document indicating Washington stayed anywhere else while in New York City.

Fraunces Tavern's illustrious history includes several devastating fires since Washington bade his officers farewell in 1783, and the building has undergone much reconstruction. It functioned variously as a U.S. government office building, an inn, storehouse, tenement, and saloon. Through part of the nineteenth century, the sign "Washington's Headquarters" hung on the building. Then, in 1907, it was purchased by the Sons of the Revolution in the State of New York and totally remodeled to its present appearance. Today, Fraunces Tavern houses a restaurant on the ground floor and a museum above.

In 1789, Samuel Fraunces joined Washington's household as steward in the presidential mansion when New York City was the nation's capital. Washington discharged Fraunces early in 1790, complaining about the steward's extravagance, but the president had second thoughts and eventually rehired him. Fraunces subsequently moved with Washington to the new capital, Philadelphia, remaining with him until 1794. Fraunces died in 1795 and is buried in Philadelphia.

Some consider Samuel Fraunces to have been a mulatto, but he is not so listed in city directories. Whites who came from the West Indies, such as Alexander Hamilton, were generally known as West Indians.

There is an apocryphal story about a young daughter of Fraunces's saving Washington's life when she uncovered an assassination plot and intercepted a plate of poisoned peas, tossing them out the window in the nick of time. (Chickens pecking in the yard supposedly died after eating them.) This story is unsubstantiated and is sometimes jumbled up with characters from another alleged conspiracy—combination of loyalists and one Thomas Hickey, an accused turncoat member of Washington's personal guard who was tried, found guilty, and hanged in New York in 1776.

Washington's remarks upon observing the infantry attacks on the Yorktown redoubts are taken from the biography of David Humphreys, an aide-de-camp at the time of the battle.

The only known detailed contemporary account of Washington's farewell in the Long Room was written by Major Benjamin Tallmadge, and is the one generally quoted by historians writing about the scene. In this book, Tallmadge's words are used here and there, without attribution.

After leaving the Long Room, Washington met for a little while with civilian dignitaries such as Governor Clinton, Mayor James Duane, and the city council. Then he exited Fraunces Tavern and walked toward the nearby Whitehall Ferry slip, passing along the paraded ranks of the troops who had marched into the city with him. The departure from New York was virtually silent, His Excellency not speaking to the onlookers. He climbed down into the boat for the trip across the Hudson River to Paulus Hook, New Jersey, and when out on the water gave a final wave of his hat to the spectators on shore.

The journey by horseback to Congress at Annapolis was slow, because everywhere Washington went he was obliged to respond to the enthusiastic greetings of the locals, in towns and cities large and small all along the route. Accompanying him on that journey were Steuben, Humphreys, and Walker—these last two would go with him to Mount Vernon. At Annapolis, just before officially submitting his resignation to Congress on December 23, 1783, Washington's last official act was to write a letter of commendation to Steuben.

Below are two noteworthy examples of Washington's attitudes toward soldiering and the war [several minor spelling errors have been corrected, others left in the style of the period].

The following, issued to the Continental Army at New York about three weeks before the Battle of Long Island and known as Washington's order on profanity, is from *The Papers of George Washington, Revolutionary War Series,* Vol. 5.

General Orders
Head Quarters, New York, August 3rd 1776.

That the Troops may have an opportunity of attending public worship, as well as take some rest after the great fatigue they have gone through; the General in future excuses them from fatigue duty on Sundays (except at the Ship Yards, or special occasions) until further orders. The General is sorry to be informed that the foolish, and wicked practice, of profane cursing and swearing (a Vice heretofore little known in an American Army) is growing into fashion; he hopes the officers will, by example, as well as influence, endeavour to check it, and that both they, and the men will reflect, that we can have little hopes of the blessing of Heaven on our Arms, if we insult it by our impiety, and folly; added to this, it is a vice so mean and low, without any temptation, that every man of sense, and character, detests and despises it.

Washington's Farewell Address to the Army
Rocky Hill, New Jersey, 2 November 1783
Draft copy, Library of Congress, Washington, D.C.,
Washington Papers.

General Washington's Farewell Orders issued to the Armies of the United States of America the 2d day of Novr 1783— Rocky Hill, near Princeton.

The United States, in Congress assembled, after giving the most honorable testimony to the Merits of the Federal Armies, and presenting them with the thanks of their Country for their long, eminent and faithful Services, having thought proper, by their Proclamation bearing date the 18th day of October last, to discharge such part of the Troops as were engaged for the War, and to permit the Officers on Furlough to retire from Service from and after tomorrow, which Proclamation having been communicated in the public papers for the information and government of all concerned, it only remains for the Commander in Chief to address himself once more, and that for the last time, to the Armies of the United States (however widely dispersed the Individuals who composed them may be) and to bid them an affectionate—a long farewell.

But before the Commander in Chief takes his final

leave of those he holds most dear, he wishes to indulge himself a few moments in calling to mind a slight review of the past, He will then take the liberty of exploring with his Military friends their future prospects, of advising the general line of conduct which in his opinion ought to be pursued, and he will conclude the Address, by expressing the obligations he feels himself under for the spirited and able assistance he has experienced from them, in the performance of an arduous Office.

A contemplation of the compleat attainment (at a period earlier than could have been expected) of the object for which we contended, against so formidable a power, cannot but inspire us with astonishment and gratitude. The disadvantageous circumstances on our part, under which the War was undertaken, can never be forgotten. The singular interpositions of Providence in our feeble condition were such, as could scarcely escape the attention of the most unobserving—where the unparalleled perseverance of the Armies of the United States, through almost every possible suffering and discouragement, for the space of eight long years was little short of a standing Miracle.

It is not the meaning nor within the compass of this Address, to detail the hardships peculiarly incident to our Service, or to describe the distresses which in several instances have resulted from the extremes of hunger and nakedness, combined with the rigors of an inclement season. Nor is it necessary to dwell on the dark side of our past affairs. Every American Officer and Soldier must now console himself for any unpleasant circumstances which may have occurred, by a recollection of the uncommon scenes in which he has been called to act, no inglorious part; and the astonishing Events of which he has been a witness—Events which have seldom, if ever before, taken place on the stage of human action, nor can they probably ever happen again.

For who has before seen a disciplined Army formed at once from such raw Materials? Who that was not a witness could imagine, that the most violent local prejudices would cease so soon, and that Men who came from the different parts of the Continent, strongly disposed by the habits of education, to dispose and quarrel with each other, would instantly become but one patriotic band of Brothers? Or who that was not on the spot can trace the steps by which such a wonderful Revolution has been effected, and such a glorious period put to all our Warlike toils?

It is universally acknowledged that the enlarged prospect of happiness, opened by the confirmation of our Independence and Sovereignty, almost exceeds the power of description. And shall not the brave Men who have contributed so essentially to these inestimable acquisitions, retiring victorious from the Field of War, to the Field of Agriculture, participate in all the blessings which have been obtained? In such a Republic, who will exclude them from the rights of Citizens and the fruits of their labours? In such a Country so happily circumstanced the pursuits of Commerce and the cultivation of the Soil, will unfold to industry the certain road to competence.

To those hardy Soldiers, who are actuated by the spirit of adventure, the Fisheries will afford ample and profitable employment, and the extensive and fertile Regions of the West will yield a most happy Asylum to those, who, fond of domestic enjoyment are seeking for personal independence. Nor is it possible to conceive that any one of the United States will prefer a National Bankruptcy and a dissolution of the Union, to a compliance with the requisitions of Congress and the payment of its just debts—so that the Officers and Soldiers may expect considerable assistance in recommencing their civil occupations from the sums due to them from the Public, which must and will most inevitably be paid.

In order to effect this desirable purpose, and to remove the prejudices which may have taken possession of the Minds of any of the good People of the States, it is earnestly recommended to all the Troops that with strong attachments to the Union, they should carry with them into civil Society the most conciliating dispositions; and that they should prove themselves not less virtuous and useful as Citizens, than they have been persevering and victorious as Soldiers. What tho' there should be some envious Individuals who are unwilling to pay the Debt the public has contracted, or to yield the tribute due to Merit, yet let such unworthy treatment produce no invective, or any instance of intemperate conduct, let it be remembered that the unbiased voice of the Free Citizens of the United States has promised the just reward, and given the merited applause, let it be known and remembered that the reputation of the Federal Armies is established beyond the reach of Malevolence, and let a consciousness of their achievements and fame, still incite the Men who composed them to honorable Actions; under the persuasion that the private virtues of economy, prudence and industry, will not be less amiable in civil life, than the more splendid qualities of valour, perseverance and enterprise, were in the Field: Every one may rest assured that much, very much of the future happiness of the Officers and Men, will depend upon the wise and manly conduct which shall be adopted by them, when they are mingled with the great body of the Community.

And altho', the General has so frequently given it as his opinion in the most public and explicit manner, that unless the principles of the Federal Government were properly supported, and the Powers of the Union increased, the honor, dignity and justice of the Nation would be lost for ever; yet he cannot help repeating on this occasion, so interesting a sentiment, and leaving it as his last injunction to every Officer and every Soldier, who may view the subject in the same serious point of light, to add his best endeavours to those of his worthy fellow Citizens towards effecting these great and valuable purposes, on which our very existence as a Nation so materially depends.

The Commander in Chief conceives little is now wanting to enable the Soldier to change the Military character into that of the Citizen, but that steady and decent tenor of behaviour which has generally distinguished, not only the Army under his immediate Command, but the different Detachments and separate Armies, through the course of the War; from their good sense and prudence he anticipates the happiest consequences; And while he congratulates them on the glorious occasion which renders their Services in the Field no longer necessary, he wishes to express the strong obligations he feels himself under, for the assistance he has received from every Class—and in every instance.

He presents his thanks in the most serious and affectionate manner to the General Officers, as well for their Counsel on many interesting occasions, as for their ardor in promoting the success of the plans he had adopted—To the Commandants of Regiments and Corps, and to the other Officers for their great Zeal and attention in carrying his orders promptly into execution—To the Staff for their alacrity and exactness in performing the duties of their several Departments—And to the Non-commissioned officers and private Soldiers, for their extraordinary patience in suffering, as well as their invincible fortitude in Action—To the various branches of the Army, the General takes this last and solemn opportunity of professing his inviolable attachment & friendship—He wishes more than bare professions were in his power, that he was really able to be useful to them all in future life; he flatters himself however, they will do him the justice to believe, that whatever could with propriety be attempted by him, has been done.

And being now to conclude these his last public Orders, to take his ultimate leave, in a short time, of the Military Character, and to bid a final adieu to the Armies he has so long had the honor to Command— he can only again offer in their behalf his recommendations to their grateful Country, and his prayers to the God of Armies. May ample justice be done them here, and may the choicest of Heaven's favors both here and hereafter attend those, who under the divine auspices have secured innumerable blessings for others: With these Wishes, and this benediction, the Commander in Chief is about to retire from service— The Curtain of separation will soon be drawn—and the Military Scene to him will be closed for ever.

ACKNOWLEDGEMENTS

The author is sincerely grateful to all those who so generously contributed their time and expertise. Thanks go to them for most of what is right in this book; the author is responsible for the rest.

First, thanks to Irene and Chris Monson, who saw the importance of telling the story of *Washington's Farewell*, and whose support made this book possible.

I am grateful once again to editor Glenn Novak for his excellent work; to Ron Toelke and Barbara Kempler-Toelke, book designers; and to Collins Sennett of Images from the Past. Thanks for help with acquiring images to Jill Hays. Thanks to Fraunces Tavern Museum director Lauren Kaminsky and staff; to Revolutionary War experts George Neumann, for an inspiring talk on Washington in the Revolution, and Ray Andrews for his generous advice. Thanks to Frank Grizzard, editor of the University of Virginia's on-line collection of George Washington's papers, and to his associate Ronda Chollock. Also thanks to Mary Ison of the Library of Congress. Thanks to New York State Library principal librarian, Lee Stanton, and his staff; and to the staff of the Chatham, New York, Public Library: Wendy Fuller, director; Carolyn Brust, and Elizabeth Gaupman. Thanks also to Katharine Westwood, supervisor of local history and genealogy at Berkshire Athenaeum, Pittsfield, Massachusetts. Thanks to Tordis Ilg Isselhardt, publisher of Images from the Past, who yet again saw the importance of an American story that needed telling in a book—one that strives to do the people of the past all honor.

As ever, with every book, thanks to my wife, Els, my first reader and partner in all of it.

SELECTED BIBLIOGRAPHY

Abbott, Wilbur C. *New York in the American Revolution.* New York: Charles Scribner's Sons, 1929.

Abbot, W.W. ed. *The Papers of George Washington.* Charlottesville: University Press of Virginia, 1983-.

Barker, W.S. *Itinerary of General Washington.* Lambertville, N.J.: Hunterdon House, 1970.

Bliven, Bruce, Jr. *Under the Guns; New York: 1775-1776.* New York: Harper & Row, Publishers, 1972.

Burnett, Robert R. "The Robert Burnett Papers." Microform. Albany: New York State Library, 1980.

Callahan, North. *General Washington's General.* New York: Rinehart & Company, 1958.

Commager, Henry S. and Richard Morris, eds. *The Spirit of Seventy-six.* New York: Harper & Row, 1974.

Davis, Burke. *The Campaign that Won America.* New York: The Dial Press, 1970.

Falkner, Leonard. *Forge of Liberty.* New York: E.P. Dutton & Co., 1959.

Fiske, John. *The American Revolution,* 2 Vols. Boston & New York: Houghton, Mifflin & Company, 1891.

Fitzpatrick, John C., ed. *Diaries of George Washington.* Washington, D.C.: U.S. Government Printing Office, 1931-.

___. *George Washington's Accounts of Expenses While Commander-in-chief of the Continental Army, 1775-1783.* Boston & New York: Houghton Mifflin Company, 1917.

Fleming, Thomas J. *Beat the Last Drum; the Siege of Yorktown, 1781.* New York: St. Martin's Press, 1963.

Flexner, James Thomas. *George Washington in the American*

Revolution. Boston: Little Brown and Company, 1967.

Freeman, Douglas S. *George Washington, A Biography*. Vol. 5. New York: Charles Scribner's Sons, 1952.

Furneaux, Rupert. *The Pictorial History of the American Revolution*. Chicago: J.G. Ferguson Publishing Company, 1973.

Hale, Edward Everett. "Nathan Hale." New Haven: The Connecticut Society of the Sons of the American Revolution, n.d.

Hastings, Hugh. *Public Papers of George Clinton*. Vol. VIII. Albany: The State of New York, 1904.

Hendrickson, Robert. *Hamilton I*. New York: Mason Charter, 1976.

Humphreys, Frank Landon. *Life and Times of David Humphreys*, 2 Vols. New York: G. P. Putnam's Sons, 1973.

Ketchum, Richard M., ed. *The Revolution*. New York: American Heritage Publishing Company, 1958.

Leake, Isaac Q., *Memoir of the Life and Times of John Lamb*. Albany: Joel Munsell, 1857.

Lossing, Benson J. *The Pictorial Field-book of the American Revolution*. New York: Harper & Brothers, 1860.

Miles, Christine, et al. *A Toast to Freedom*. New York: Fraunces Tavern Museum, 1984.

Moore, Frank. *Diary of the American Revolution*. New York: Washington Square Press, 1967.

Morris, Richard B., ed. *Alexander Hamilton and the Founding of the Nation*. New York: The Dial Press, 1957.

Murray, Stuart. *The Honor of Command—General Burgoyne's Saratoga Campaign*. Bennington: Images from the Past, 1998.

O'Callaghan, E.B. *The Documentary History of the State of New York*, Vols. 1 and 8. Albany: Weed, Parsons & Co., 1850.

Palmer, John McAuley. *General von Steuben*. New Haven: Yale University Press, 1937.

Pennypacker, Morton. *General Washington's Spies*. Brooklyn: Long

Island Historical Society, 1939.

Pierce, Melusina Fay. "The Landmark of Fraunces Tavern: a retrospective." New York: Printed for the Women's Auxiliary of the American Scenic and Historic Preservation Society, ca. 1901.

Quincy, Josiah. *The Journals of Major Samuel Shaw.* Boston: Wm. Crosby & H. P. Nichols, 1847.

Randall, Willard Sterne. *Benedict Arnold.* New York: Quill, 1990.

Rice, Kym S. *Early American Taverns.* New York: Fraunces Tavern Museum, 1983.

Riker, James. "Evacuation Day, 1783." New York: Privately printed, 1883.

Rubenstein, Anita. *The Public Career of Nicholas Fish.* Ann Arbor: University Microfilms International, 1982.

Scheer, George F. and Hugh F. Rankin, eds. *Rebels and Redcoats.* Cleveland: World Publishing Company, 1957.

Tallmadge, Benjamin. *Memoir of Col. Benjamin Tallmadge.* New York: Arno Press, 1968.

Thane, Elswyth. *Washington's Lady.* Mattituck, N.Y.: Aeonian Press, 1977.

SOURCES OF ILLUSTRATIONS

Cover: The Library of Congress, Washington, DC.

ix, 10, 19, 34, 35, 48, 50-51, 56, 74, 83, 86-87, 119, 132-33, 142, 176, 202-03: various including *American Portrait Gallery,* Lillian Buttre, J.C. Buttre, New York, 1877; *The American Revolution* Vol. 1, John Fiske, Houghton, Mifflin & Co., Boston and New York, 1896; and *The National Cyclopedia of American Biography;* Vol I, George Derby, Editor, J.T. White & Co., New York, 1893.

Frontispiece, 28-29, 73: *Public Papers of George Clinton.* Vol VIII, Hugh Hastings, State of New York, Albany, 1904.

6-7: *The Story of the Greatest Nations and The World's Famous Events* Vol IX, Edward S. Ellis and Charles F. Horne, Francis R. Niglutsch, New York, 1913, 1914.

12, 20, 21, 23, 138, 191, 194, 213: *Pictorial Field Book of the Revolution* Vol II, Benson J. Lossing, Harper & Brothers, New York, 1852.

24: *1776: The Adventure of the American Revolution,* Irving Werstein, Cooper Square Publishers, Inc., NY, 1973.

42, 224-25: Fraunces Tavern Museum, New York City.

60, 96-97, 199: *The History of Our Country*, Edward S. Ellis, The Jones Brothers Publishing Co., Cincinnati and Henry W. Knight, New York, 1895.

78, 110-11, 182: *The American Revolution: A Picture Sourcebook,* John Grafton, Dover Publications, Inc., New York, 1975.

104: *The Journals of Major Samuel Shaw,* Wm. Crosby & H.P. Nichols, Boston, 1847.

148-49, 220-221: *The Life and Times of Washington,* John F. Schroeder, Johnson, Fry, and Co., New York, 1857.

INDEX

Note: Illustrations are shown using *italicized* page numbers

IMAGES FROM THE PAST

Publishing history in ways that help people
see it for themselves
Other of our books you might enjoy

ALLIGATORS ALWAYS DRESS FOR DINNER:
An Alphabet Book of Vintage Photographs
By Linda Donigan and Michael Horwitz

A collection of late 19th- and early 20th-century images from around the world reproduced in rich duo tone for children and all who love historical pictures. Each two-page spread offers a surprising visual treat: Beholding Beauty—a beautifully dressed and adorned Kikuyu couple; Fluted Fingers—a wandering Japanese Zen monk playing a bamboo recorder; and Working the Bandwagon—the Cole Brothers Band on an elaborate 1879 circus wagon. A-Z information pages with image details.

9 1/4" x 9 3/4", 64 pages ISBN 1-884592-08-2
Cloth $25.00

LETTERS TO VERMONT **Volumes I and II:**
**From Her Civil War Soldier Correspondents
to the Home Press**
Donald Wickman, Editor/Compiler

In their letters "To the Editor" of the Rutland Herald, young Vermont soldiers tell of fighting for the Union, galloping around Lee's army in Virginia, garrisoning the beleaguered defenses of Washington, D.C., and blunting Pickett's desperate charge at Gettysburg. One writer is captured, another serves as a prison camp guard, others are wounded—and one dies fighting in the horrific conflict in the Wilderness of Virginia. Biographical information for each writer (except one who remains an enigma) and supporting commentary on military affairs. 54 engravings and prints, 32 contemporary maps, 45 historical photographs. Extensive index.

Vol. 1, 6" x 9", 251 pages ISBN 1-884592-10-4
Cloth $30.00   ISBN 1-884592-11-2   Paper $19.95

Vol. 2, 6" x 9", 265 pages ISBN 1-884592-16-3
Cloth $30.00   ISBN 1-884592-17-1   Paper $19.95

REMEMBERING GRANDMA MOSES
By Beth Moses Hickok

Grandma Moses, a crusty, feisty, upstate New York farm wife and grandmother, as remembered in affectionate detail by Beth Moses Hickok, who married into the family at 22, and raised two of Grandma's granddaughters. Set in 1934, before the artist was "discovered", the book includes family snapshots, and photographs that evoke the landscape of Eagle Bridge, home for most of her century-plus life. Two portraits of Grandma Moses—a 1947 painting and a 1949 photograph, and nine historical photographs. On the cover is a rare colorful yarn painting given to the author as a wedding present.

6" x 9", 64 pages ISBN 1-884592-01-5 Paper $12.95

REMAINS UNKNOWN
By Michael J. Caduto with sixteen pencil sketches by Adelaide Murphy Tyrol

He somehow found his way to Vermont soon after the Mexican War. It was a long journey, the beginning of a private purgatory that lasted over 150 years. At last, with the help of friends he'd never met, he took the final steps in a quiet cemetery by the river on a sultry afternoon.

In this strange and haunting tale, based on a true story, the reader enters a world suspended between our earthly existence and the realm of the human spirit. A small community of people embarks on an adventure that compels them to bring the mysterious, mummified remains of one long dead to a resting place of peace and grace. With help from two distinct spiritual traditions, and a dose of healing humor in the face of grief, the journey unfolds with a sense of dignity and compassion.

5" x 7", 80 pages ISBN 1-884592-24-4   Cloth $15.00

AMERICA'S SONG: The Story of Yankee Doodle
By Stuart Murray

During the first uncertain hours of the Revolution, British redcoats sang "Yankee Doodle" as an insult to Americans - but when the rebels won astounding victories this song of insult was transformed to a song of triumph, eventually becoming "America's Song."

This is the first complete chronicle of the story of "Yankee Doodle," perhaps the best-known tune in all the world. From its early days an ancient air for dancing, through the era of Dutch and Puritan colonial settlement, "Yankee Doodle" evolved during the French and Indian Wars and the American Revolution to become our most stirring anthem of liberty.   Index. Bibliography. Illustrated with 37 prints and maps.

5" x 7", 248 pages ISBN 1-884592-18-X Cloth $21.00

RUDYARD KIPLING IN VERMONT:
Birthplace of The Jungle Books
By Stuart Murray

This book fills a gap in the biographical coverage of the important British author who is generally described as having lived only in India and England. It provides the missing links in the bitter-sweet story that haunts the portals of Naulakha, the distinctive shingle style home built by Kipling and his American wife near Brattleboro, Vermont. Here the Kiplings lived for four years and the first two of their three children were born.

All but one of Kipling's major works stem from these years of rising success, happiness and productivity; but because of a feud with his American brother-in-law, which was seized on by newspaper reporters eager to put a British celebrity in his place, the author and his family left their home in America forever in 1896.

6" x 9"; 208 pages; Extensive index. Excerpts from Kipling poems, 21 historical photos; 6 book illustrations; and 7 sketches convey the mood of the times, character of the people, and style of Kipling's work.

ISBN 1-884592-04-X Cloth $29.00 ISBN 1-884592-05-8 Paper $18.95

THE HONOR OF COMMAND:
Gen. Burgoyne's Saratoga Campaign
By Stuart Murray

Leaving Quebec in June, Burgoyne was confident in his ability to strike a decisive blow against the rebellion in the colonies. Instead, the stubborn rebels fought back, slowed his advance and inflicted irreplaceable losses, leading to his defeat and surrender at Saratoga on October 17, 1777—an important turning point in the American Revolution. Burgoyne's point of view as the campaign progresses is expressed from his dispatches, addresses to his army, and exchanges with friends and fellow officers; 33 prints and engravings, 8 maps, 10 sketches. Index

7" x 10", 128 pages ISBN 1-884-592-03-1 Paper $14.95

NORMAN ROCKWELL AT HOME IN VERMONT:
The Arlington Years, 1939-1953
By Stuart Murray

Norman Rockwell painted some of his greatest works, including "The Four Freedoms" during the 15 years he and his family lived in Arlington, Vermont. Compared to his former home in the suburbs of New York City, it was "like living in another world," and completely transformed his already successful career as America's leading illustrator. For the first time he began to paint pictures that "grew out of the every day life of my neighbors."

32 historical photographs, 13 Rockwell paintings and sketches, and personal recollections. Index. Regional map, selected bibliography, and listing of area museums and exhibitions.

7" x 10", 96 pages ISBN 1-884592-02-3 Paper $14.95

THE ESSENTIAL GEORGE WASHINGTON: **Two Hundred Years of Observations on the Man, Myth and Patriot**
By Peter Hannaford

Why did Thomas Paine turn against him? Why did Martha Bland call him "impudent"? What is the truth about the cherry tree story? What was his single most important quality? These and many more questions about the man called "the father of his country" are answered in this collection. The reader meets Washington's contemporaries, followed by famous Americans from the many decades between then and now and, finally, well-known modern-day Americans. Included are Benjamin Franklin, Thomas Jefferson, Abigail Adams, Parson Weems, Abraham Lincoln, Walt Whitman, Woodrow Wilson, Bob Dole, George McGovern, Eugene McCarthy, Letitia Baldrige, Newt Gingrich, Ronald Reagan—and many more. Read in small doses or straight through...either way, the book gives a full portrait of the man who—more than any other—made the United States of America possible. Over 60 prints and photographs.

5" x 7", 200 pages ISBN 1-884592-23-6 Cloth $19.50

Available at your local bookstore or from Images from the Past, Inc., 888-442-3204 for credit card orders; P.O. Box 137, Bennington, Vermont 05201 with check or money order. When ordering, please add $4.00 shipping and handling for the first book and $1 for each additional. (Add 5% sales tax for shipments to Vermont.) www.ImagesfromthePast.com